Mark

Tansey

'A Modest Proposal', 1975
Gouache auf Postkarte / *gouache on postcard*
140 x 90 mm, Privatsammlung / *Private
collection*, Courtesy Gagosian Gallery, New York

Mark

Museum Kurhaus Kleve, 23.1.-24.4.2005 / Württembergischer Kunstverein Stuttgart, 4.5.-17.7.2005

Tansey

Kerber Verlag

Inhalt / *Contents*

Leihgeber / *Lenders*

The Broad Art Foundation, Santa Monica,
  Kalifornien / *California*
Daros Collection, Schweiz / *Switzerland*
Gagosian Gallery, New York
Collection Danielle and David Ganek
Collection Donald B. Marron, Lightyear Capital,
  New York
Privatsammlung / *Private collection*, Courtesy
  Gagosian Gallery
The Schroeder Collection
Mark Tansey, New York

Vorwort

6 Durch seine Teilnahme an der documenta 8, 1987, wurde Mark Tansey in Europa schlagartig bekannt. In einer Zeit, in der die europäischen 'Neuen Wilden' mit Vehemenz an einer neuen Malerei arbeiteten, wirkten seine Gemälde mit ihrer reduzierten Farbigkeit, ihrem erzählerischen Charakter und ihren photorealistisch ausformulierten Details auf den ersten Blick höchst befremdlich. Fast alle Bilder zeigen weite Landschaften, in denen rätselhafte Begegnungen stattfinden – figürliche Kompositionen, die trotz geradezu anekdotischer Detailgenauigkeit keineswegs leicht lesbar sind. Soldaten, Forscher oder fremde Volksstämme treffen mit ihren Werkzeugen oder Vehikeln aufeinander. Vielfach umgeben von Feuer, Wasser, Luft oder Erde finden die dargestellten Szenen wie auf einer Bühne statt. Die komplexe und konzeptuelle Anordnung der Motive ist in der Malerei des 20. Jahrhundert, ohnegleichen. Tanseys historische und philosophische Kenntnis, sein Interesse für die Geschichte des Mediums Malerei und die Lust an allegorischen Kompositionen erinnern an Nicolas Poussin, an Caspar David Friedrich oder im Bereich der zeitgenössischen Kunst an Jeff Wall.

Die jeweils in der Skala eines einzigen Farbtons gemalten Bilder – Grisaillen, Brunaillen, 'Bleuaillen' ... – wirken wie nach Photographien gemalt, scheinbare Dokumentationen eines historischen Ereignisses, das jedoch niemals stattgefunden hat, das allein der Phantasie des Malers entstammt und von ihm als Konzentrat einer Erfindung oder Entwicklung in einer metaphernreichen Szene zugespitzt wird. Wissenschaftliche Theorien, künstlerischer Richtungsstreit oder aktuelle gesellschaftliche Themen werden in Tanseys Bildern abgehandelt und verwandelt. Es sind kollektive Erinnerungsbilder, die der Maler in seiner unverwechselbaren, aber schwer entzifferbaren Sprache präsentiert. Historisch gekleidete Personen bevölkern die Gemälde, deren Rätselhaftigkeit sie in die Nähe des Surrealismus rückt.

Tatsächlich handelt es sich um eine virtuose, aber bewusst einfach gehaltene Malerei mit surreal anmutenden Szenen, die Tanseys profunden Kenntnissen der Geistes- und Kunstgeschichte entspringen und zurückzuführen sind auf sein

Foreword

Through his participation in *documenta 8* in 1987, Mark Tansey became known in Europe vitually overnight. At that time, when Europe's neo-Expressionists were vehemently working on a new kind of painting, Tansey's paintings, with their monochromatic colours, their narrative character and their photorealistic details seemed very strange at first glance. Almost all of his paintings depict vast landscapes in which enigmatic confrontations take place – figural compositions which, despite their precise, anecdotal attention to detail, are very difficult to comprehend. Soldiers, research scientists or strange tribes confront each other with their tools and/or vehicles. Surrounded by fire, air, earth and water, Tansey's scenes are reminiscent of theatrical tableaux. The complex, conceptual arrangement of the motifs is unparalleled in 20th century painting. Tansey's knowledge of history and philosophy, his interest in the history of painting and the delight he takes in allegorical compositions remind one of Nicolas Poussin, Caspar David Friedrich or, in the contemporary context, Jeff Wall.

Painted in the tonal values of a single colour – grisaille, brunaille, 'bleuaille' ... –, Tansey's paintings look as though they have been painted from photographs, like documentations of historical events. But they are events that have never taken place, events that are purely the figment of the artist's imagination and depicted in richly metaphorical scenes as concentrated forms of an idea or development. Scientific theories, artistic disputes or current social issues are thematicized and transformed in Tanseys' paintings. They are paintings of collective memory which Tansey presents in his unmistakable yet barely decipherable language. People in historical dress populate his paintings, the enigmatic character of which immediately awakens associations with Surrealism.

Indeed, Tansey's works are distinguished by a style of painting which is both virtuose and deliberately simple, their surrealistic scenes deriving from a profound knowledge of the history of art and philosophy and fed from an immense archive of

immenses Archiv von Bildern aller Art. Was in seinen Gemälden über die Hürden der Zeit miteinander zum neuen Bild verwächst, findet seinen Ursprung zunächst als Collage, in der Tansey seine Bildquellen ausschöpft und über den Photokopierer homogenisiert. Die Bilder der letzten Jahre sind in einem leuchtenden Ultramarin gehalten, einer Farbe, die der neuen, seit 2002 entstandenen Werkgruppe gleichermaßen etwas Tiefes wie auch etwas Leichtes verleiht.

Mit dieser Diskrepanz ist das Wesentliche von Mark Tanseys Kunst umschrieben. Der Künstler präsentiert komplexe und vielschichtige Inhalte in der Verpackung einer präzise beschreibenden und zugleich meisterhaften Malerei. Seine großen Bilder sind eine Herausforderung für die Betrachter, denen der Künstler viel abverlangt. Sie begeben sich auf eine Reise in vergangene Zeiten, die besonders diejenigen genießen, denen das Bildpersonal schon einmal begegnet ist und die sich nicht zum ersten Mal mit europäischer oder amerikanischer Geschichte und den daraus resultierenden Geschichten befassen.

Berühmt wurde Mark Tansey durch sein Gemälde 'Triumph of the New York School' von 1984, heute im Whitney Museum, New York, in dem er die Diskussion um den Primat in der Kunst in Anlehnung an Velázquez' Meisterwerk 'Die Übergabe von Breda' (Las Lanzas) auf den Punkt bringt. Eine Gruppe Soldaten in französischen Uniformen aus dem Ersten Weltkrieg trifft auf eine Gruppe amerikanischer Soldaten in Uniformen aus dem Zweiten Weltkrieg. Die Dargestellten lassen sich leicht identifizieren: Angeführt von André Breton stehen Picasso, Duchamp, Matisse und viele andere den amerikanischen Künstlern Rothko, de Kooning, Pollock etc. unter der Führung des Kunstkritikers Clement Greenberg gegenüber. Breton unterschreibt die Kapitulation: 'Amerika übernimmt das Kommando' war 1999 der Titel einer großen Übersichtsausstellung amerikanischer Kunst nach dem Zweiten Weltkrieg im Whitney Museum.

Die neuen Bilder, wie 'West Face', 'Trio', 'Sea Change', 'Wake', 'Snowman' und 'Duet', die nun erstmals in Europa zu sehen sind, zeigen wiederum weite Landschaften, die mittlerweile jedoch weniger als zeitlose Bühne und Hinter-

---

images. What in his paintings seems to blend harmoniously together in spite of all the obstacles of time begins as a collage, this being exhaustively composed from all kinds of pictorial material and then homogenized with the aid of a photocopying machine. Tansey's paintings of the last few years are executed in a brilliant ultramarine blue, a colour which lends his new group of paintings, begun in 2002, a quality of both depth and lightness.

It is precisely this discrepancy which is the essential mark of Tansey's art. The artist packages highly complex subject matter in accurately descriptive and technically masterful paintings. His large paintings are a challenge to the viewer, for they make heavy demands on him. They take him on a journey into times gone by, a journey which is particularly enjoyable for those who are able to recognize the persons depicted and are already familiar with European and American history and the events that ensued.

Mark Tansey became famous through his painting 'Triumph of the New York School' of 1984, now owned by the Whitney Museum, New York. The theme of the painting is the struggle for supremacy in art, which Tansey treats by drawing an analogy with Velázquez's masterpiece 'The Surrender of Breda' (Las Lanzas). A group of soldiers in French uniforms from the First World War stands opposite a group of American soldiers in uniforms from the Second World War. The persons depicted are easily identifiable: standing behind their leader André Breton are Picasso, Duchamp, Matisse and many other representatives of the European avant-garde; the Americans, led by the art critic Clement Greenberg, include Rothko, de Kooning and Pollock. Breton is signing the treaty of surrender: 'America Takes Command' was the title of a large exhibition on American post-war art mounted at the Whitney Museum in 1999.

Tansey's latest paintings, such as 'West Face', 'Trio', 'Sea Change', 'Wake', 'Snowman' and 'Duet', which are now being exhibited in Europe for the first time, again feature vast expanses of landscape, but now they serve not as a timeless setting and background for the happenings in the painting but, rather, as the central motif, into which Tansey's references – to

grund für das Geschehen fungieren, sondern die das zentrale Bildmotiv darstellen und in die die geistesgeschichtlichen Verweise förmlich eingeschrieben sind. So bilden Berge und Täler Schnittstellen für zwei gleichzeitig anwesende Motive, wenn zum Beispiel Schnee, Steine und Schatten auf der einen Seite die ornamentale Oberfläche eines Bergrückens bilden und zugleich bei näherem Hinsehen ein Gesicht markieren. Diese so integrierten Gesichter sind anamorphotische Porträts von Philosophen, und zwar von Denkern, die für Tansey das moderne Leben prägen. Je nach Porträt entwickelt sich die gemalte Landschaft so zu einem Bild für das Ideale, das Existentielle oder das Fragmentarische.

Das Werk von Mark Tansey hat sich mitten in New York recht abgeschlossen von der Öffentlichkeit entwickelt. Erstmals in Deutschland wird es nun in einer umfassenden Einzelausstellung gezeigt. Neben den neuen Bildern werden auch einige frühe Arbeiten präsentiert, so dass die Entwicklung des Werkes anschaulich gemacht wird. Die Ausstellung bietet die einmalige Gelegenheit, einen der wichtigsten amerikanischen Maler, der in Europa noch nicht den Bekanntheitsgrad erlangt hat, der seiner Bedeutung entspricht, kennen zu lernen.

Dem Künstler, Mark Tansey, gilt unser großer Dank: für seine Bereitschaft, seine Werke in Kleve und Stuttgart auszustellen, für seine Hilfe und für sein großes Engagement. Besonders möchten wir hervorheben, dass der Künstler aus seinem persönlichen Besitz die als Entwürfe für seine Bilder zu betrachtenden Collagen beigesteuert hat. Die Besucher der Ausstellung erhalten so einen einzigartigen Einblick in den Prozess der Bildfindung des Künstlers, der essentiell für das Verständnis von Tanseys Malerei ist.

Dass diese Ausstellung zustande kam, ist Dr. Roland Mönig, Kustos am Museum Kurhaus Kleve, zu verdanken, der schon vor mehreren Jahren Mark Tansey eingeladen und mit großer Geduld und Energie das Ausstellungsprojekt vorangetrieben hat. Er hat Ausstellung und Katalog betreut und mit seinem Text einen profunden Beitrag zum Werk von Mark Tansey verfasst. Ihm gilt unser Dank ebenso wie Daniela Goeller, die einen kurzen, konzentrierten Text über Tanseys frühe Arbeiten beisteuerte.

---

the history of art, thought etc. – are quite literally integrated. Mountains and valleys serve as the interfaces for different motifs which are present in the painting at one and the same time. This is the case, for example, when snow, rocks and shadows simultaneously form the structure of a mountain ridge and, upon closer scrutiny, a human face. These integrated faces are anamorphotic portraits of philosophers – philosophers who for Tansey have left their mark on modern life. Depending on the portrait, the painted landscape evolves into an expression of the real, the existential, the fragmentary. Mark Tansey's oeuvre has developed in relative seclusion, in the middle of New York, well away from the public eye. His works are now being shown for the first time in Germany in a comprehensive one-man exhibition. Tansey's new paintings are accompanied by some of his earlier works, thus enabling the viewer to form a picture of the artist's development. The exhibition represents a unique opportunity to view the works of one of America's most important painters, a painter who in Europe has not yet attained the fame that his significance warrants.

We are deeply indebted to Mark Tansey both for his willingness to exhibit his works in Cleves and Stuttgart and for his help and enormous commitment. Particularly deserving of mention is the fact that the artist has contributed from his own personal collection almost all of the collages that served as the studies for his paintings. Thus the visitor to the exhibition will be afforded a unique insight into the artist's way of working and, by the same token, will receive essential guidance towards an understanding of Tansey's painting.

For the exhibition itself, we owe our thanks to Dr. Roland Mönig, Curator of the Museum Kurhaus Kleve. His invitation to Mark Tansey was made several years ago and since then he has been working on this exhibition project with enormous patience and energy. He has been responsible for both the exhibition and the catalogue and his essay makes a profound contribution to the existing literature on Mark Tansey's oeuvre. Our thanks also go to Daniela Goeller for her short yet concentrated text on Tansey's early works.

Many people have contributed to the realization of this pro-

Viele haben zur Realisierung der Ausstellung beigetragen. Die Gagosian Gallery in New York und ihr Direktor John Good mit seinen Mitarbeitern Molly Klais, Alison McDonald und Tom Pilgrim haben uns mit Rat und Tat zur Seite gestanden, viele Fragen geklärt und Probleme gelöst, ebenso wie Mark Tanseys Assistentin Rebecca Lawton.

Besonderer Dank gilt den Leihgebern in den Vereinigten Staaten, in England und der Schweiz, waren sie doch bereit, uns für die Dauer der Ausstellung ihre kostbaren, teils soeben erst erworbenen Bilder anzuvertrauen.

Um ein so großes Projekt verwirklichen zu können, waren wir auf großzügige Unterstützung angewiesen. Die Erarbeitung und Realisierung der Ausstellung in Kleve wurde gefördert durch die Kulturstiftung des Bundes und die Kunststiftung NRW, die so die große Bedeutung des Projekts für Deutschland und Nordrhein-Westfalen betont haben. Der Direktorin der Kulturstiftung des Bundes, Hortensia Völckers, sowie der Präsidentin und der Generalsekretärin der Kunststiftung NRW, Ilse Brusis und Regina Wyrwoll, möchten wir für diese Hilfe sehr herzlich danken. Auch die Botschaft der Vereinigten Staaten hat die Bedeutung der Ausstellung durch ihre Förderung unterstrichen. Botschafter Daniel R. Coats, Kulturattaché Richard Aker und Generalkonsul George Knowles haben auf diese Weise dem amerikanisch-deutschen Kulturaustausch auf schöne Weise Ausdruck verliehen.

Die Präsentation in Stuttgart wurde gefördert durch die Stiftung Landesbank Baden-Württemberg und die Hugo Boss AG. Dadurch wurde es uns als neuer Leitung des Württembergischen Kunstvereins ermöglicht, mit einem besonderen 'Highlight' zu beginnen.

Wir wünschen den Lesern des Buches und den Besuchern der Ausstellung Konzentration und Aufmerksamkeit für das Werk von Mark Tansey und seine großartige Malerei.

Guido de Werd
Museum Kurhaus Kleve

Iris Dressler / Hans D. Christ
Württembergischer Kunstverein Stuttgart

---

ject. The Gagosian Gallery in New York and its Director John Good, along with his members of staff Molly Klais, Alison McDonald and Tom Pilgrim, have given us every moral and practical support, clarified many a query and solved many a problem, as has Mark Tansey's assistant Rebecca Lawton, to whom we are equally indebted.

A special word of thanks goes to those collectors in the United States, the United Kingdom and Switzerland who have been prepared to part with their precious 'Tanseys' – some of which have only just been purchased – and place them in our care for the duration of the exhibition.

Such a large project could not have been realized without generous financial support. The preparations and realization of the exhibition in Cleves were sponsored by the Federal Cultural Foundation and the Arts Foundation of North Rhine-Westphalia, both of which have stressed the enormous significance of this project for Germany and North Rhine-Westphalia. The Director of the Federal Cultural Foundation, Hortensia Völckers, and the Director and General Secretary of the Arts

Foundation of North Rhine-Westphalia, Ilse Brusis and Regina Wyrwoll, deserve our wholehearted thanks. The Embassy of the United States, too, has underscored the significance of this exhibition through its financial support. Daniel R. Coats, Ambassador to Germany, Richard Aker, Cultural Attaché and Consul General George Knowles have in this way given wonderful expression to the notion of German-American cultural exchange.

The exhibition in Stuttgart has been sponsored by the Landesbank Baden-Württemberg Foundation and Hugo Boss AG. Thus it has been possible for Iris Dressler and Hans D. Christ, as the new directors of the Württembergischer Kunstverein, to start off with a really special 'highlight'.

We wish the readers of this catalogue and all visitors to the exhibition much concentrated enjoyment with the oeuvre of Mark Tansey and his magnificent painting.

Guido de Werd
Museum Kurhaus Kleve

Iris Dressler / Hans D. Christ
Württembergischer
Kunstverein Stuttgart

Das Bild schaut zurück *Roland Mönig*

10   Es ist eine hochgradig absurde Versuchsanordnung, beschrieben mit größtmöglicher Sachlichkeit: Eine Kuh steht im Saal eines Museums und wird hier mit einem (leicht verfremdeten) Gemälde des niederländischen Tiermalers Paulus Potter konfrontiert, das zwei ihrer Artgenossen zeigt. Zu beiden Seiten des Bildes im Bild stehen bebrillte Bewohner des kunsthistorischen Elfenbeinturms mit schütterem Haar, die die Reaktionen der Kuh auf das soeben enthüllte Gemälde beobachten und protokollieren. Wird das Tier überhaupt auf die Malerei ansprechen? Und wenn ja: Wird es die Repräsentation der Wirklichkeit für die Wirklichkeit selbst nehmen? Oder wird es nur Formen und Farben ohne Zusammenhang erkennen?

Mark Tanseys Bild 'The Innocent Eye Test' ist gehalten in nur einem einzigen zurückhaltenden Sepia-Ton und wirkt auf den ersten Blick wie die Wiedergabe einer historischen Photographie – eine Assoziation, mit der die eigentümlich altmodische, vage an die 1940er und 1950er Jahre erinnernde Kleidung der Figuren zusammenstimmt. Tatsächlich handelt es sich um ein komplexes, durch und durch konstruiertes Sinn-Bild, das einen der zentralen Glaubenssätze der frühen Moderne revidiert und ironisiert: die Vorstellung von der Unschuld des Auges. Sie geht zurück auf John Ruskin, der schrieb, J.M.W. Turners Malerei gelinge es, das wieder zu beleben, was man die 'Unschuld des Auges' nennen könne – 'a sort of childish perception of these flat stains of colour merely as such, without consciousness of what they signify'[1]. Kunsthistorisch bedeutsam wurde Ruskins Wort von der 'Unschuld des Auges' (der Monet'sche Heuhaufen am rechten Rand von Tanseys Komposition weist darauf hin) insbesondere für die Bewertung impressionistischer Kunst, von Werken mithin, in denen die Farbe autonomisiert, die Form aufgelöst und – unabhängig vom Motiv – der Akt der Wahrnehmung selbst zum Thema gemacht wird. Von hier aus ließ sich das Argument mühelos bis weit ins 20. Jahrhundert hinein verlängern – über die abstrakte bzw. gegenstandslose und konkrete Kunst der Klassischen Moderne bis hin zum Minimalismus und zu Frank Stellas Losung: 'What you see is what you see'.

The Picture Looking Back *Roland Mönig*

It is an extremely absurd experimental set-up, described with the greatest possible objectivity: a cow stands in the room of a museum and is confronted with a (slightly alienated) painting by the Dutch animal painter Paulus Potter depicting two other members of its species. Standing on either side of this painting-within-a-painting are several bespectacled, thin-haired occupants of this art-historical ivory tower who are carefully observing and recording the cow's reactions to the just unveiled painting. Will the cow react at all? And, if so, will it see this representation of reality as reality itself? Or will it merely recognize shapes and colours without making any connection between them?

Mark Tansey's painting, 'The Innocent Eye Test' is executed in a subdued sepia tone that awakens associations, at first glance, with a historical photograph – an association entirely in keeping with the peculiarly old-fashioned dress of the depicted figures, this being vaguely reminiscent of the 1940s and 1950s. The painting is in fact a complex, altogether ironizing allusion to one of the central doctrines of early modernism: the notion of the innocence of the eye. Its origin goes back to John Ruskin, who wrote of Turner's paintings that they succeeded in reviving what one might call the 'innocence of the eye' – 'a sort of childish perception of these flat stains of colour merely as such, without consciousness of what they signify'[1]. In particular, Ruskin's notion of the 'innocence of the eye' was an art-historically important criterion for the appreciation of Impressionist art (the Monet-style haystack at the right-hand edge of Tansey's painting alludes to this) and in general for those works in which colour was autonomous, forms were dissolved and – regardless of the motif – the act of perception itself became the subject matter. From there the argument could be prolonged well into the 20th century – via the abstract, non-representational and concrete art of classic modernism to Minimalism and Frank Stella's slogan: 'What you see is what you see'.

Studie zu / *Study for* 'Triumph of the
New York School', 1984
Öl auf Leinwand / *oil on canvas*
107 x 168 cm, Mark Tansey, New York

Zweifellos besitzt die Kuh – ein Sinnbild für Ruhe und Gleichmut, wenn nicht für Gleichgültigkeit – jenes unschuldige Auge, welches die Apologeten einer selbstbezüglichen Kunst und des reinen Sehens zum Ideal erheben. Zugleich freilich geht ihr alles intellektuelle Vermögen und auch die unabdingbare Fähigkeit zur Selbstreflexion ab. Sie besitzt nicht einmal genug Bewusstsein, um im Angesicht der Kunst ihre Blasen- und Darmfunktionen zu zügeln. Den Wissenschaftlern, die sie für ihr Experiment in den makellos weißen Kubus des Museums versetzt haben, ist das selbstverständlich klar. Ein Mann am linken Bildrand hält einen Wischmopp in der Hand, um nötigenfalls rasch zu beseitigen, was das Tier unter sich gehen lässt.

Der 1981 entstandene 'Innocent Eye Test', heute im Besitz des Metropolitan Museum of Art, New York, zählt zu den frühen Höhepunkten von Mark Tanseys Werk, das sich seit dem Ende der 1970er Jahre als kritische Antwort auf das gebetsmühlenartig wiederholte Diktum vom Tod oder Ende der Malerei entwickelte[2]. Seine Arbeiten zeichnen sich aus durch einen eigentümlich trockenen, gleichsam dokumentarischen Stil, der an wissenschaftliche Illustrationen erinnert. Ein überbordendes Bildarchiv speist die Imagination des Künstlers. Es enthält Abbildungen aus Zeitungen und Magazinen, Reproduktionen aus Kunstbüchern und Fachzeitschriften sowie eigene Photographien. Das visuelle Rohmaterial wird mit Hilfe des Kopierers zu Collagen verarbeitet, in denen die Komposition der Leinwände erprobt und festgelegt werden kann – ein minutiöser Prozess, bei dem die Tätigkeit der Hand und die Tätigkeit des Geistes gleichberechtigt sind. Wenn schon das wiederholte Kopieren der Vorlagen eine erste Vereinheitlichung der aus disparaten Quellen stammenden Bildelemente bewirkt, so verschleift die malerische Umsetzung auch noch die letzten Brüche und beruhigt und homogenisiert den Bildraum. Eine wesentliche Rolle spielt dabei die Monochromie. Sie erlaubt es, das gegenständliche Bild als 'conjectural field' zu definieren – als einen Ort, an dem Unmögliches möglich wird und Gedanken, Thesen, Fiktionen überprüft werden können[3].

Als Mark Tansey seine ersten Gemälde schuf, ging es ihm zunächst darum,

The cow – a symbol of contentment and equanimity, if not to say indifference – is undoubtedly blessed with that innocent eye which the apologists of self-reflexive art and pure seeing have made their ideal. Admittedly, the cow lacks every intellectual capacity and also the absolutely indispensable ability for self-reflection. Indeed, the cow does not even possess enough self-awareness to be able to control her bodily functions. For the scientists, who have placed the cow in the immaculately white cube of the museum, this is a foregone conclusion: one of the men on the left is holding a mop at the ready, just in case the cow leaves anything behind.

'The Innocent Eye Test', painted in 1981 and now owned by the Metropolitan Museum of Art, New York, is one of the early highlights of Mark Tansey's oeuvre. Since the end of the 1970s, Mark Tansey has been reacting critically to the parrot-fashion repeated dictum of the death or end of painting[2]. His works are distinguished by a peculiarly dry, virtually documentary style reminiscent of scientific illustrations. The artist feeds his imagination from a picture archive overflowing with photographs from newspapers and magazines, reproductions from art books and scientific and technical journals as well as his own photographs. This visual raw material is processed with the aid of a photocopier into collages which then enable the artist to try out and determine the compositions for his canvases – a painstaking process in which the activity of the hand and the activity of the brain enjoy equal rights. While the repeated copying of the disparate picture elements achieves only an initial uniformity of image, the ultimate painterly execution on canvas smoothes the edges and covers the cracks, tranquillizing and homogenizing the picture space. An important role in this process is played by the use of monochrome. It permits definition of the representational image as a 'conjectural field' – as a place where the impossible becomes possible and ideas, thoughts, theories and fictions can be checked[3].

When Mark Tansey first began painting, he was concerned primarily with rehabilitating the figurative image and redefining the task of representation. To this end, in one programmatic work after another, Tansey went through all the de-

das figürliche Bild zu rehabilitieren und die Aufgabe der Repräsentation neu begründen, und so deklinierte er in programmatischen Arbeiten die Ge- und Verbote einer puristischen, vom Geist der Abstraktion durchdrungenen Moderne durch. Es folgten Bilder über Bilder – allegorische Kompositionen, die mit Hintersinn und Ironie von den Konzepten und Theorien der unterschiedlichen Avantgarden des 20. Jahrhunderts handeln. Die Leistungen von Protagonisten der europäischen Kunst wie Cézanne, Picasso, Braque, Duchamp und Malewitsch werden dabei ebenso rekapituliert wie die Positionen der 'Abstract Expressionists' in Amerika. Auf einer Reihe von Bildern rufen Soldaten in den Monturen des Ersten und Zweiten Weltkriegs in Erinnerung, was das Wort 'Avantgarde' ursprünglich bezeichnete, nämlich die Vorhut der kämpfenden Truppe, die als erste in Feindesland eindrang. Sicherlich am effektivsten spielt 'Triumph of the New York School' (1984) mit der militärischen Metapher: Vor dem noch rauchenden Schlachtfeld kapitulieren die Vertreter der École de Paris vor den mit Macht aufstrebenden Abstrakten Expressionisten der amerikanischen Ostküste.

In der zweiten Hälfte der 1980er Jahre bezog Mark Tansey wichtige Impulse aus der Philosophie des französischen Strukturalismus und Dekonstruktivismus, insbesondere aus den Schriften von Jean Baudrillard, Roland Barthes und Jacques Derrida. Alle drei erscheinen (bemerkenswerter Weise inmitten einer Gruppe sich entkleidender Soldaten) auf dem Hauptwerk 'Mont Sainte-Victoire' (1987) – einem monumentalen Gemälde, das zwei zentrale Motive Paul Cézannes, nämlich das titelgebende Gebirgsmassiv in der Provence und die Badenden, mit Platons erkenntnistheoretischer Metapher der Höhle verschränkt. In der Folge galt Tanseys Interesse verstärkt der Frage, wie Bild und Bedeutung, Wahrnehmung und Interpretation miteinander zusammenhängen, was schließlich auch zur Einbeziehung von Buchstaben und gesiebdruckten Textfragmenten in seine Arbeiten führte. In Bildern wie 'Close Reading' (1990) verwandelt Text sich unversehens in Textur, stehen die Zeilen einer Buchseite ein für die Schichten des Sedimentgesteins. Parallel und ergänzend zu den von der französischen Philosophie angeregten Untersuchungen zur Relation zwischen Bild und Text

---

clensions of the dos and don'ts of a purist, abstraction-oriented modernism. There then followed paintings about paintings – allegorical compositions thematicizing with much subtlety and irony the concepts and theories of all the many different avant-gardes of the 20th century. The accomplishments of such protagonists of European art as Cézanne, Picasso, Braque, Duchamp and Malevich were recapitulated just as much as those of the Abstract Expressionists in America. In a whole series of paintings, soldiers in the uniforms of the First and Second World Wars remind us of the original meaning of the French word 'avant-garde' (English 'vanguard'), namely the foremost of an army, the first to penetrate the enemy lines. A painting which plays effectively with this military metaphor more than any other is 'Triumph of the New York School' (1984): against the background of a still smoking battlefield, the exponents of the École de Paris capitulate to the ever more powerful Abstract Expressionists from the American East Coast.

During the second half of the 1980s, Mark Tansey was influenced by a great many important impulses from the philoso-

phies of French structuralism and deconstructivism, and especially from the writings of Jean Baudrillard, Roland Barthes and Jacques Derrida. All three of them appear (remarkably in the middle of a group of soldiers who are in the process of undressing) in Tansey's main work 'Mont Sainte-Victoire' (1987), a monumental painting which merges two of Paul Cézanne's favourite themes, namely the massif in Provence which gives this painting its title and the Bathers, with Plato's epistemological metaphor of the cave. There then followed a period of deep preoccupation with the question of the relationship between image and meaning, between perception and interpretation, a thought process which ultimately led to the incorporation of letters of the alphabet and silk-screened textual fragments in his works. In paintings like 'Close Reading' (1990), text suddenly metamorphoses into texture, the lines of text from the page of a book taking the place of the strata of a sedimentary rock. Both in parallel and in synergism with his French philosophy-inspired investigations into the relationship between image and text, Tansey devoted a lot of his time

beschäftigte Tansey sich mit fraktaler Geometrie sowie mit den Denkmodellen der Chaos- und Komplexitätstheorie. Insofern sie das Augenmerk auf Bewegungen, Übergänge, Texturen lenken, stellen sie sozusagen eine wissenschaftliche Entsprechung zu seinem bildnerischen Denken dar. Die Arbeiten der folgenden Jahre zeigen die Welt der Erscheinungen im Fluss, sind erfüllt von einer geradezu filmisch wirkenden Dynamik, die Landschaften und Figuren gleichermaßen erfasst und Verformungen und Verwandlungen unterwirft – ein Titel wie 'Transition Team' (1997) ist in dieser Hinsicht bezeichnend.

In vieler Hinsicht verfolgt Mark Tansey mit seiner jüngsten, seit 2000 in zahllosen Collagen und Studien vorbereiteten Werkgruppe, aus der dieser Katalog erstmals Arbeiten zeigt, konsequent Fragestellungen weiter, die seine Arbeit seit dem Ende der 1970er Jahre geprägt haben. Zugleich schlägt er mit ihr ein ganz neues Kapitel in seinem Schaffen auf. Äußerlich sind die Bilder der letzten Jahre schon dadurch als eng zusammengehörig erkennbar, dass sie durchweg in Ultramarin gemalt sind, einer Farbe, die in Tanseys Œuvre bisher nicht vorkam. Das Ultramarin sprach ihn an, weil es einerseits die Tiefe und Subtilität des Schwarz haben kann und andererseits die Leichtigkeit und Transparenz des Blau. Die Sujets der neuen Gemälde sind im besten Sinn des Wortes elementar: Wasser, Schnee, Wolken, Felsen. Es handelt sich um Landschaften, die, wie Mark Tansey selbst sagt, 'all figurative' sind: von Figuren erfüllt, von Figuren belebt, teils sogar aus Figuren gebildet. Auf diesen Leinwänden ist alles in Bewegung – auf der motivischen wie auf der semantischen Ebene. Wer sich mit ihnen befasst, muss deshalb ebenfalls in hohem Maße beweglich sein, und zwar sowohl körperlich als auch geistig. Um die großformatigen Bilder in ihrer ganzen Komplexität erfassen zu können, muss der Betrachter vor und zurück treten, muss immer wieder die Distanz suchen, um sich ihnen dann aufs Neue zu nähern. Und jedes Mal, wenn der Blick sich einstellt, verändert sich zwangsläufig sowohl die Einschätzung der Komposition als Ganzer wie auch die Deutung ihrer einzelnen Bestandteile und deren innerer Beziehung zueinander. Der Dialog mit diesen Gemälden kann niemals abgeschlossen, sondern nur abge-

---

to fractal geometry and the hypotheses of the chaos and complexity theories. Insofar as they concern movements, transitions and textures, these theories are, so to speak, the scientific equivalent of his visual thinking. The works painted by Mark Tansey in the years that followed depict a world of phenomena in flux; they are filled with a filmic dynamism that animates figures and landscapes alike, subjecting them to distortion and transformation – a work like 'Transition Team' (1997) is a typical one in this context.

In many respects, Mark Tansey's cycle of works produced since 2000 from countless collages and studies – a selection of which is illustrated for the first time in this catalogue – consistently pursues those questions that have dominated his work since the end of the 1970s. At the same time, however, it marks the beginning of a new chapter in his oeuvre. Outwardly, Mark Tansey's paintings of the last few years are obviously closely related, not least through the fact that they are all painted in ultramarine blue, a colour that Tansey has never used before. Ultramarine blue appealed to him because, on the one hand, it can have the depth and subtlety of black and, on the other, the lightness and transparency of blue. The subject matter of Tansey's new paintings is, in the best sense of the word, elementary: water, snow, clouds, rocks. They are landscapes which, as Mark Tansey himself says, are 'all figurative': filled with figures, enlivened with figures, and to a certain extent even shaped from figures. On these canvases everything is in motion – both in terms of form and in terms of content. The viewer must thus be equally mobile, both physically and mentally. In order to read these large-format paintings in their entire complexity, one must constantly step backwards and forwards, looking at them from a distance and then at close quarters. And immediately one's eye is focused, the way one sees the composition as a whole changes completely, as does one's interpretation of its individual elements and the way they relate to each other inwardly. Thus the dialogue with these painting can never end, but only be interrupted. To quote Mark Tansey: 'What a work of art is about unfolds in the eye-mind-hand-material process and is carried on in the viewer's

brochen werden. Mit Mark Tansey gesprochen: 'What a work of art is about un-folds in the eye-mind-hand-material process and is carried on in the viewer's rea-ding. It's more like a process of questioning and performing than capturing.'[4]

Niemals waren Tanseys Arbeiten einfach zu lesen, und immer rechneten sie damit, dass das Bewusstsein des Betrachters mit Bildern aller Art gesättigt ist. Sie boten Anspielungen, die es zu entschlüsseln, komplexe Codes, die es zu de-chiffrieren galt. Die Werke der letzten Jahre aber gehen noch einen entschei-denden Schritt weiter, denn sie verweigern sich jeder geradlinigen oder einsin-nigen Interpretation. Sie zu betrachten heißt, eine Vielzahl von Perspektiven und Sinnangeboten miteinander zu verknüpfen, ohne jemals zu einer defini-tiven Deutung zu gelangen. Figur ist Grund, Grund ist Figur, das Eigentliche ist das Uneigentliche, und das Uneigentliche ist das Eigentliche – alles kann po-tentiell auch etwas anderes sein oder sich in etwas anderes verwandeln. Wahr-heit ist eine schwebende Größe und blitzt auf allein im Übergang von einer Deutung zur nächsten. Tanseys jüngste Arbeiten konfrontieren den Betrachter mit unauflösbaren Rätseln, ziehen ihn nolens volens hinein in einen Strudel aus Assoziationen und Empfindungen. Seine Erfahrungen vor dem Bild sind notwendiger Bestandteil des Bildes selbst. Exemplarisch möchte ich das an-hand von drei Gemälden näher erläutern: 'Wake' (2003), 'West Face' (2004) und 'Snowman' (2004).

Das in etwa quadratische Format von 'Wake' wird ganz und gar bestimmt vom Wasser, von seinem Strömen und rhythmischen Wogen sowie von den gleißen-den Reflexen, die das Licht der tief stehenden Sonne auf ihm erzeugt. Tanseys Malerei bildet das Wasser nicht einfach nur ab, sie hat seine besonderen Quali-täten in sich aufgenommen, hat sie in eine vibrierende Textur von hoher Sinn-lichkeit übersetzt. Wo der Betrachter eigentlich steht, wie er sich gegenüber der senkrecht vor ihm aufgeklappten Wasseroberfläche verorten soll, bleibt unklar. Es gibt keine eindeutigen Bezugspunkte, an denen er sich orientieren könnte und die es ihm erlauben würden, sein Verhältnis zum imaginären Raum der Darstellung zu bestimmen. Links im Vordergrund verspricht ein klassisch an-

---

reading. It's more like a process of questioning and perform-ing than capturing.'[4]

Tansey's paintings have never been easy to read, and they have always reckoned with the fact that the viewer's conscious-ness is filled to overflowing with all kinds of images. They have always confronted the viewer with allusions that had to be de-ciphered, cryptic codes that had to be broken. The paintings of the last few years, however, go a big step further in that they defy all straightforward or one-way interpretation. Viewing them entails the linking together of a multitude of perspec-tives and offered meanings without ever arriving at a definite interpretation. Figure is ground, ground is figure, the essential is the inessential, and the inessential is the essential – every-thing can potentially be something else or metamorphose into something else. The light of truth is an unsteady variable that flashes only for the moment of transition from one interpre-tation to the next. Tansey's most recent works confront the viewer with unsolvable riddles, plunge him willy-nilly into a maelstrom of associations, emotions and sensations. What

the viewer experiences as he stands in front of the painting is essentially part and parcel of the painting itself. I should like to exemplify this by the three paintings, 'Wake' (2003), 'West Face' (2004) and 'Snowman' (2004).

The more or less square format of 'Wake' is totally domi-nated by water, by its current, by the rhythm of its waves, by its glistening reflections of light from a sun low down on the horizon. However, Tansey's painting does not simply depict the water, but has absorbed its particular qualities, too, trans-lating them into a vibrantly sensuous texture. Exactly where the viewer is meant to stand in front of this vertically tipped expanse of water is not at all clear. There are no definite points of reference which might help him to orient himself or enable him to relate physically to the imaginary picture space of the painting. Depicted in the left foreground in the position of a classical repoussoir is the iron railing of a platform, which at first glance promises to be a helpful guide but is, in the final analysis, only an added irritant. This zigzagging railing ends abruptly, and its tall corner post supports a striped awning

mutendes Repoussoir, dem Blick Halt und Sicherheit zu geben, aber tatsächlich vermehrt es nur die Irritationen. Das im Zickzack verlaufende schmiedeeiserne Geländer bricht unversehens ab, und der auf ihm ruhende Pfosten trägt eine Markise, die wie ein Vexierbild vor und zurück zu springen scheint, als konvexe wie als konkave Form verstanden werden kann. Im Unterschied zu früheren Arbeiten löst Tansey hier die aus der Collage unterschiedlicher kopierter Bildvorlagen sich ergebenden Brüche und Widersprüche ganz bewusst nicht vollständig auf.

Der Titel 'Wake' lenkt die Aufmerksamkeit auf das zentrale Motiv des Bildes: auf das scharf konturierte Kielwasser eines Motorbootes, das mit großer Geschwindigkeit die vertikal entlang der Mittelsenkrechten verlaufende Spiegelung des Sonnenlichtes kreuzt. Es ist zweifellos der stärkste Indikator für Zeit und Vergänglichkeit in dieser Arbeit, in der alles zu fließen und sich aufzulösen scheint. Der Titel gibt überdies einen Hinweis darauf, was am linken unteren Rand der Komposition geschieht. Dort hat sich unter Markise und Sonnenschirm eine Festgesellschaft aus elegant gekleideten Frauen und Männern versammelt. Auf einem runden Tisch in ihrer Mitte stehen zahlreiche im Gegenlicht suggestiv aufleuchtende Gläser. Zwei Pokale haben sich wie von Geisterhand erhoben und schweben frei im Raum – ein irreal-phantastisches Detail, das den rituellen Charakter der Szene unterstreicht und die Anwesenden als Zelebranten ausweist. Es handelt sich um einen 'wake', einen Leichenschmaus, wie er in Irland traditionellerweise nach einer Beerdigung gefeiert wird. Die Dargestellten sind Angehörige und Freunde der Familie Tansey; auch Mark Tansey selbst ist darunter. Der 'wake', den sie feiern, gilt dem 1998 verstorbenen Vater des Künstlers. Er gehört zu den halb im Schatten versinkenden Passagieren an Bord des Schnellbootes, das nun als jene Fähre kenntlich wird, die der antiken Mythologie zufolge die Seelen der Verstorbenen ins Jenseits bringt. Das Gewässer, auf dem sie fährt, mag ebenso der Styx wie der Hudson oder (wenn man den französischen Schriftzug auf dem Sonnenschirm bedenkt) die Seine sein. Ein erstaunlicher Kontrapunkt zum dahinrasenden Boot ist der rechts

---

which, like an optical illusion, seems to be visible either from above or below, either as a concave or as a convex form. Here, contrary to his earlier works, Tansey has deliberately left some of the visual incompatibilities and contradictions resulting from the collaging process completely unresolved.

The title 'Wake' automatically draws attention to the central motif of the painting, namely the sharply contoured, horizontal wake of a speed-boat crossing the vertical reflection of the sunlight in the water. This is undoubtedly the most obvious reference to time and transience in a work in which everything is in a state of flux and change. The title also hints at what is taking place in the bottom left-hand corner of the painting. Gathered there under the awning and a sunshade is a group of festively dressed men and women. On a round table in their midst are numerous glasses sparkling suggestively against the light. Two of them are hovering freely in a space, as if held by invisible hands – a totally unreal, phantasmagorial detail which underscores the ritualistic, celebratory mood of the scene, for this is where the word 'wake' takes on its other

meaning. The figures in the painting are relatives and friends of the Tansey family. Mark Tansey himself is among them. The traditional Irish wake being celebrated here is that of the artist's father who died in 1998. He is one of the passengers in the speed-boat which, as it disappears into the evening shadows, we now clearly recognize as that ferry of ancient mythology transporting the souls of the dead to the underworld. Whilst the waters they are crossing might be those of the River Styx, they could just as easily be the waters of the River Hudson or – if we go by the French logo on the sunshade – the waters of the River Seine. An astonishing counterpoint to the rapidly disappearing speed-boat is the football bobbing up and down on the choppy water in the bottom right-hand corner of the painting. Its sheer banality clashes with the solemnity of the wake and seems to indicate 'end of game'[5].

Turning our gaze back to the wake of Charon's ferry, and upon closer examination thereof, we discover the anamorphic portrait of the young James Joyce. The author of 'Finnegans Wake', now dead for over sixty years, is 'awake' again, brought

unten in den Fluten treibende Fußball. Mit seiner Banalität bricht er die Feierlichkeit des 'wake' und scheint anzuzeigen: 'end of game'[5].

Ins Kielwasser von Charons Fähre ist, wie sich bei genauer Betrachtung zeigt, ein anamorphotisches Porträt des jungen James Joyce eingeschrieben. Der 1941 gestorbene Verfasser von 'Finnegans Wake' ist 'awake', erwacht zu neuem Leben in einer Komposition, die von Vergänglichkeit und Tod handelt. Gewiss muss man darin zunächst eine sehr persönliche Hommage von Mark Tansey an seinen Vater sehen, einen Mann, dem die Werke des irischen Dichters so viel bedeuteten. Tansey nennt ihn denn auch liebevoll einen 'Joycean Catholic'.

Darüber hinaus ist nicht von der Hand zu weisen, dass die ästhetischen Strategien Mark Tanseys und die literarischen Errungenschaften von James Joyce einander gleichsam spiegelbildlich entsprechen. Wenn Joyce mit 'Finnegans Wake' einen Roman schuf, der keinen Anfang und kein Ende hat, der niemals endgültig zu interpretieren (und demzufolge auch nicht zu übersetzen) ist, der 65 Weltsprachen zu einem neuen, vor Anspielungen überbordenden Idiom amalgamiert, so führt Tansey Bilder unterschiedlichster Provenienz zusammen, stiftet offene, spannungsreiche Beziehungen zwischen ihnen und macht damit das Sprechen und Schreiben über seine Arbeit zu einer Herausforderung. Von 'Finnegans Wake' ist gesagt worden, es sei ein Buch, das man eigentlich nur anschauen, nicht aber 'lesen' könne[6]. Umgekehrt gilt, dass man eine Arbeit wie Mark Tanseys 'Wake' nicht nur anschauen, sondern auch lesen, d.h. nach und nach in allen Einzelheiten ihrer Motive und ihrer Textur erforschen muss. Sobald der Blick eintaucht in die Malerei, multiplizieren sich im Wechselspiel von Figur und Grund die Bilder – und damit auch die nicht zu beantwortenden Fragen: ein Porträt von Charles Darwin scheint ebenso auf wie groteske Fratzen, die an die Cartoons von Kindern oder auch an Hieronymus Bosch erinnern, und am oberen Rand der Komposition formieren sich vermeintlich disparate Flecken zu mehreren ineinander geblendeten Frauenköpfen. Aus Wellen werden Gesichter und wieder Wellen. Es ist, als trete man ein in einen 'stream of consciousness', habe teil am ungebundenen Wandern eines Geistes, das sich in Farbe materiali-

---

back to life in a composition that has death and transience as its theme. We must of course see this reference to James Joyce first and foremost as Mark Tansey's personal homage to his father, a man to whom the works of the Irish writer meant so much. Tansey endearingly refers to his father as a 'Joycean Catholic'.

It cannot be denied, however, that Mark Tansey's and James Joyce's strategies – the former artistic, the latter literary – operate in a similar way. While James Joyce's 'Finnegans Wake' has neither a beginning nor an end, defies unequivocal interpretation (and hence translation) and amalgamates sixty-five languages of the world into a new idiom brimming over with allusions, Mark Tansey combines images from the widest diversity of sources, openly relates them to one another and, in so doing, makes all attempts at talking or writing about his work a veritable challenge. 'Finnegans Wake' is said to be a book that one can actually only look at, but not 'read'.[6] Conversely, a work like Mark Tansey's 'Wake' must not only be looked at but also read, that is to say, the viewer must explore it little by little, paying careful attention to every detail of its motifs and texture. But as soon as the viewer's gaze plunges into the painting, the images multiply in a confusing interaction of figure and ground and, by the same token, give rise to a multiplicity of unanswerable questions: now a portrait of Charles Darwin looms into view, then grotesquely hideous faces reminiscent of children's cartoon characters or figures in a painting by Hieronymus Bosch, and, at the top edge of the composition, seemingly disparate patches of colour suddenly form several intermerging women's heads. Waves turn into faces and then back into waves. It is as though one is being carried along in a 'stream of consciousness', as though one is partaking in the unhindered wanderings of a mind that have materialized into colour. And then the viewer suddenly realizes that he is being observed as he 'reads' the painting: one of the figures under the sunshade has raised his glass to his eye, like a telescope, and focused it on the viewer.

At first glance, 'West Face' seems to be about an alpine adventure. Running parallel to the picture plane is a range of

siert. Und plötzlich erkennt man, dass man beim Sehen / Lesen beobachtet wird: Eine der Figuren unter dem Sonnenschirm hat sein Glas wie ein Fernrohr erhoben und fokussiert den Betrachter.

Bei 'West Face' scheint es sich zunächst um die Schilderung eines Hochgebirgsabenteuers zu handeln. Parallel zur Bildfläche verläuft eine Kette von schneebedeckten Berggipfeln mit steilen Abstürzen, schroffen, dunkel hervortretenden Felsgraten und bedrohlich klaffenden Gletscherspalten. Überhöht wird die Wirkung der Landschaft in ihrer elementaren Wucht noch durch die dramatisch über ihr sich auftürmenden Wolken, auch sie wahre Gebirge, allerdings erfüllt von Licht und Bewegung. Im Vordergrund kämpft sich eine Gruppe von schwer bepackten Wanderern durch den tiefen Schnee, während neben ihr drei Bergsteiger verzweifelt versuchen, im Widerstand gegen den eiskalten Wind ein Zelt aufzuschlagen. Eine dritte Gruppe Menschen hat den Berg bereits zur halben Höhe erklommen. Insbesondere bei der Umsetzung des Schnees, der unter den energischen Tritten der Wanderer aufbricht und dessen verharschte Oberfläche zu Schollen zerfällt, zeigt sich erneut die Meisterschaft von Tanseys Malerei. Indem der Künstler mit einem scharfen Gegenstand in die noch feuchte Farbe kratzt und die weiße Grundierung der Leinwand freilegt, lässt er die materiellen Qualitäten des Schnees geradezu mit Händen greifbar werden. Mit einer weiteren, lasierend aufgetragenen Schicht weißer Farbe suggeriert er den Eisnebel, der die Beine der Bergsteiger umweht und ihre Konturen mit zunehmender Distanz verwischt.

Wer aus der Überschau in die Nahsicht wechselt, wer 'West Face' in seinen Details liest und eindringt in den komplexen Text des Bildes, erkennt bald, dass dessen Thema – bei aller Präzision in der Wiedergabe einer Hochgebirgsexpedition mit ihren spezifischen Härten – eigentlich ein ganz anderes ist. Wie schon in 'Wake', in dessen Wellen zahllose Gesichter aufscheinen, ist auch hier die Landschaft selbst in weiten Teilen aus Figuren gebildet. Es erweist sich, dass das, was man auf den ersten Blick und mit Recht für Stein, Schnee und Eis hielt, tatsächlich menschliche Köpfe und Gestalten sind. Teils sind sie so stark verein-

---

snow-covered mountain peaks with steep precipices, dark, forbidding ridges and menacing crevasses. The sheer elemental force of this landscape is further heightened by the dramatically billowing clouds above it. They, too, are veritable mountains, albeit filled with light and movement. A group of heavily laden mountaineers struggles through the deep snow in the foreground, while not far from them three other mountaineers desperately attempt to pitch a tent in the face of an icy gale. A third group of mountaineers has already climbed half way up the mountainside. Especially Tansey's treatment of the snow, the crisp crust of which breaks into clumps under the feet of the mountaineers, demonstrates his mastery as a painter. By scratching the still wet paint with a sharp implement in order to reveal the white ground of the canvas, Tansey renders the material properties of the snow almost tangible. An additional layer of transparent white suggests the icy mist which envelops the legs of the mountaineers and blurs their contours more and more as they move into the distance.

If, after contemplating the painting from a distance, the viewer now approaches 'West Face' for a close-up view and begins to read its details, and thus becomes absorbed in its complex text, he will soon realize that its theme – in spite of the precision with which Tansey has depicted the alpine expedition and its peculiar hardships – is a completely different one. As in 'Wake', where faces are half-hidden in the waves, the landscape in 'West Face' contains similar surprises. It turns out that what the viewer at first glance thought – and quite rightly thought – to be rocks, snow and ice are in fact human heads and figures. In some parts of the painting they are so simplified and so drastically reduced to contrasts of light and dark that the relationship between figure and ground is totally and continually confused. Some of them are anamorphically distorted so as to form the contours of the rock faces and precipices.[7]

Allowing his eye to wander upwards along the route taken by the mountaineers, continuing up the flank of the mountain, the viewer will first encounter a large portrait of Friedrich

facht und so entschieden auf den Kontrast von Hell und Dunkel reduziert, dass Figur und Grund sich in einem unabschließbaren Wechselspiel befinden und immer wieder ineinander umschlagen; teils erscheinen sie zudem in anamorphotischer Verzerrung und definieren so Abhänge und Steilwände.[7]

Lässt der Betrachter von 'West Face' sein Auge an der Reihe der Bergsteiger entlang die Flanke des Berges hinaufwandern, so trifft er zunächst auf ein großes, schräg in die Fläche gedrücktes Porträt von Friedrich Nietzsche, dessen buschige Augenbrauen und gewaltiger Schnauz unverkennbar sind. Nietzsche, dessen alter ego Zarathustra die Berge als adäquaten Lebensraum des mit Weitblick begabten Denkers pries, scheint damit endlich am Ziel seiner Sehnsüchte angelangt zu sein. Die über seinem Scheitel aufsteigenden Felswände enthalten zahllose friesartig gereihte Figuren, die sozusagen von den Kräften der Gebirgsbildung zusammengedrückt worden sind. Man meint, sonntägliche Spaziergänger in einem Park erkennen zu können, unter ihnen – wie ein Leitmotiv, das 'Wake' und 'West Face' verbindet – wiederum James Joyce. Auf der nächsten Etappe der Wanderung begegnet man dem anamorphotischen Bildnis Ludwig Wittgensteins, an dessen Wange der zwar kleine, aber außerordentliche plastische Porträtkopf Karl Poppers angesetzt ist. Als Pragmatiker der Antipode Nietzsches, wendet Wittgenstein seinen Kopf in die entgegen gesetzte Richtung. Hat man das von ihm bestimmte Plateau passiert, beginnt der härteste Abschnitt des Aufstiegs zum Gipfel. Er führt von Marx, Engels und Lenin über die Vertreter des englischen Empirismus, französischen Rationalismus und deutschen Idealismus und über Existenzialisten, Strukturalisten und Dekonstruktivisten schließlich steil aufwärts zum Dreigestirn der antiken Philosophie: zu Aristoteles, Platon und Sokrates. Neben ihnen blickt ein klassisches griechisches Profil auf die Büste des Homer – Urbild des Epikers und geistiger Vorfahre von James Joyce.

Die Komposition von 'West Face' ist bei weitem zu vielschichtig, um sie mit wenigen Worten vollständig zu beschreiben und ihre intellektuelle Reichweite auszumessen. Denn indem Mark Tansey die Besteigung der Westflanke eines

---

Nietzsche pressed obliquely into the rock face, clearly recognizable by his bushy eyebrows and huge moustache. Nietzsche, whose alter ego Zarathustra lauded the mountains as the ideal Lebensraum for the far-sighted thinker, seems to have reached the ultimate goal of his yearnings. The walls of rock rising above his head contain countless figures in a frieze-like row compressed, as it were, by the immense forces exerted by the rock forming process. One is reminded of Sunday strollers in a park – and among them, as a leitmotif common to both 'Wake' and 'West Face', is James Joyce. Moving on, the viewer's eye then encounters the anamorphic portrait of Ludwig Wittgenstein and, adjacent to the latter's cheek, the small but extraordinarily three-dimensional portrait of Karl Popper. As a pragmatist and the exact reverse of Nietzsche, Wittgenstein faces in the opposite direction. Once the viewer has negotiated the plateau formed by Wittgenstein's head, the hardest part of the ascent to the summit begins. It takes him from Marx, Engels and Lenin, past the exponents of English empiricism, French rationalism and German idealism, steeper still past existentialists, structuralists and deconstructivists and then on to the triumvirate of ancient philosophy: Aristotle, Plato and Socrates. Next to them is a classical Greek profile, its gaze contemplating a bust of Homer, the very epitome of the epic poet and the intellectual ancestor of James Joyce.

The content of 'West Face' is far too complex for anyone to be able to describe it completely in just a few words or to gauge its intellectual reach. Indeed, in depicting the ascent of the west flank of a mountain, Tansey also quite literally lends facial expression to the history of Western thought. It is no accident, for example, that a map of the European Mediterranean region, the cradle of our civilization, peels itself out of the bottom right-hand corner of the painting. Taking place directly above it is a surprising exchange of positive and negative forms: stepping out of a gaping crevasse, a French soldier energetically points the way upwards and forwards with his right arm, calling to mind those Tansey paintings of the 1980s that interpreted modernism as a quasi-military vanguard. Here, in 'West Face', Tansey interprets the intellectual energies of phi-

Berges darstellt, umreißt er buchstäblich auch das Antlitz der westlichen Geistesgeschichte. Folgerichtig schält sich in der rechten unteren Ecke des Bildes aus dem Schnee eine Karte des europäischen Mittelmeerraumes als der Wiege unserer Zivilisation heraus. Direkt darüber kommt es zu einem überraschenden Austausch positiver und negativer Formen: Aus einer klaffenden Felsspalte tritt ein französischer Soldat hervor, der mit dem rechten Arm energisch bergauf weist. Er ruft Tanseys Bilder der 1980er Jahre in Erinnerung, die die Moderne als quasi-militärisches Kommandounternehmen deuten. In 'West Face' zeigt Tansey die geistigen Energien der Philosophie als physisch wirksame Naturkräfte. Eine gegenständliche Malerei, die sich an ihnen misst, wird zwangsläufig zum Extremsport. Die Bergsteiger stellen insofern ebenso sehr Identifikationsangebote für den Betrachter dar wie Figurationen des Künstlers. Sie verkörpern den kämpferischen Willen zum Aufstieg in jedem Sinne, zum Vorstoß in unbekanntes Terrain. 'It's agony vs. agon', wie Tansey sagt[8]: Der Impuls zur Tat steht gegen die Gefahr des Absturzes, den Schmerz des Scheiterns.

Im Falle von 'West Face' muss der Blick des Betrachters die Komposition erwandern und sich an den Widerständen der rauen Gebirgslandschaft reiben, bei 'Wake' schwimmt er gleichsam in einem Strom aus malerischen Notationen, in dem Bilder auftauchen, um sogleich wieder zu versinken. Beide Arbeiten setzen ein Gegenüber voraus, das bereit ist, sich intellektuell und emotional voll einzubringen und Teil eines offenen Prozesses zu werden, der mit der Arbeit des Künstlers an den ersten Collagen begann. 'Snowman' radikalisiert diesen Ansatz, denn es ist ein Bild, das den Betrachter anschaut und so die Rollen von Rezipient und Rezipiertem umkehrt.

Nähert man sich der Arbeit von weitem, so nimmt man zuerst die Form eines großen Auges wahr, das einen mit seiner dunklen Pupille fixiert. Erst aus kürzerer Entfernung ist es möglich, die disparaten Einzelheiten zu benennen, die mit stupender Stimmigkeit diesen Gesamteindruck erzeugen. Es handelt sich um eine winterliche Landschaft, die sich entlang eines Waldsaumes diagonal von links vorn nach rechts hinten entfaltet. Die tiefenräumliche Wirkung der sich

losophy in terms of the physical forces of nature. Any representational painting that is a match for them is indeed one of the most extreme of sports. Thus the mountaineers are just as much stand-ins for the viewer as they are representations of the artist and his endeavours. They embody the spirited will to climb to the top in every sense, to venture into unknown territory. 'It's agony vs. agon,' Tansey says[8]: the urge to act is held in balance by the risk of falling, the pain of failure.

While in 'West Face' the viewer's gaze must wander over the composition and negotiate the obstacles of the rough mountain landscape, in 'Wake' it floats, as it were, in a stream of painterly notations in which images suddenly appear and then disappear just as suddenly. Both of these works presuppose a viewer who is prepared to become fully involved in them and to be a part of that open-ended process which began when Tansey made his first collages. 'Snowman', on the other hand, radicalizes this process of involvement, for it is a painting which looks back at us and thus reverses the roles of the viewer and the viewed.

Slowly approaching this work from a distance, the viewer first perceives a large eye, its dark pupil fixed on him in a constant stare. Not until he is quite close to the painting is he able to discern and identify the disparate details which together form the entire image with such astonishing homogeneity. The painting depicts a wintry landscape which unfolds diagonally along the edge of a wood from bottom left to top right. The effect of depth created by the perspective of the trees is counteracted both by the artificial snow spurting out of a snow cannon in a high arc and by the sunlight which shines through it. The long shadows of the bare tree trunks on the snow-covered ground heighten the impression of flatness still further. Standing slightly to the right, just below that dark, circular part of the landscape near the centre of the canvas which forms the pupil of the apparent eye, is a second, smaller snow cannon, and to the left of it are a woman and several children busy rolling a huge snowball. Sitting in the foreground, on the left, is a fallen snowboarder, and to the right, in a hollow, countless criss-crossing wheel tracks testify to bustling activity.

verjüngenden Bäume wird konterkariert zum einen durch den im hohen Bogen aus einer Schneekanone heraustiebenden Kunstschnee und zum anderen durch das diesen durchleuchtende Licht der Sonne. Die langen Schatten der kahlen Stämme auf dem schneebedeckten Boden unterstützen noch die flächige Lesart des Bildes. Rechts unterhalb jener dunklen kreisförmigen Partie nahe der Leinwandmitte, die die Pupille des scheinbaren Auges bildet, steht eine zweite, kleinere Schneekanone, und links davon sind eine Frau und einige Kinder damit beschäftigt, eine mächtige Schneekugel zu rollen. Im Vordergrund sitzt links ein gestürzter Snowboarder, und rechts in einer Senke zeugen zahlreiche einander kreuzende Wagenspuren von hektischer Betriebsamkeit.

Der Betrachter und das Bild, das Große und das Kleine, der Raum und die Fläche, das Natürliche und das Künstliche, das Warme und das Kalte, das Vertraute und das Fremde – alle diese Dualitäten stehen in 'Snowman' in einem unauflösbaren Spannungsverhältnis. Die Figuren im Mittelgrund modellieren einen Schneemann, aber der Schnee ist wiederum selbst ein Mann: Er trägt die Züge von Karl Marx, wobei dessen Bart in paradoxer Folgerichtigkeit von einem der die Kugel rollenden Kinder gebildet wird. Der Begründer des Historischen Materialismus ist mithin selbst formbare Materie geworden. Im Bild herrscht Winter, und es sollte kalt sein, doch der Schnee muss künstlich erzeugt werden und die beim Bau des Schneemanns sich abmühende Frau trägt sportliche Sommerkleidung. Es handelt sich um eine Szene, mit der man Freizeit und Vergnügen assoziiert – aber sowohl der gestürzte Snowboarder als auch die Wagenspuren deuten auf etwas Unheilvolles, Bedrohliches hin. Wie immer man die Komposition betrachtet, sie schaut auf wieder andere Weise zurück. Einem Film vergleichbar ist alles in Bewegung, und es scheint, als sei die Schneekanone ein Projektor – ein Licht- und Bildwerfer.

In gewisser Weise kann man 'Snowman' als eine Antwort auf 'The Innocent Eye Test' auffassen, das zu Anfang der 1980er Jahre Tanseys Ruhm mitbegründete. Nicht mehr die Kuh im Bild ist es, deren Auge auf seine Unschuld geprüft wird, sondern das Publikum vor dem Bild. Es muss sich beständig fragen, was

---

Viewer and painting, large and small, space and surface, depth and flatness, natural and artificial, warm and cold, familiar and foreboding – all these dualities stand in an irresolvable relationship of tension to one another. The figures in the middle ground are building a snowman, but the snow itself is a man: his features are those of Karl Marx and his beard is formed, paradoxically yet logically, from one of the children who are rolling the snowball. This founder of historical materialism has himself become formable material. The bare trees in the painting suggest a winter scene, which ought to be cold, and yet the snow has to be made artificially and the woman building the snowman is dressed in summer sportswear. Whilst it is a scene which one readily associates with leisure and pleasure, the fallen snowboarder and the wheel tracks hint at something ominous and menacing. No matter how one looks at this composition, it always looks back at one in yet another way. As in a film, everything is in motion, with the snow cannon as the projector – of light and images.

In a certain sense, 'Snowman' may be seen as an answer to 'The Innocent Eye Test', which contributed to Tansey's rise to fame at the beginning of the 1980s. It is no longer the cow inside the painting whose eye is being tested for its innocence, but rather the members of the public outside the painting. They must constantly ask themselves what they are looking at, how they are looking at it and how they evaluate what they see. And they must also be clearly aware that they themselves are being constantly observed. The situation seems particularly precarious because 'Snowman' also contains details that are extremely topical and highly charged politically. The shadows on the left-hand edge of the hollow in the foreground, for example, suddenly metamorphose into the anamorphic portrait of the American president George W. Bush. It also appears as a reflection in the goggles of the snowboarder. Further scrutiny reveals, on the opposite side of the hollow, between the crossed wheel tracks, the head of Ahmed Chalabi, the former favourite of the US administration following the fall of Saddam Hussein. We immediately realize that there may be yet

es sieht, wie es sieht und wie es das Gesehene bewertet. Und es muss sich darüber im Klaren sein, dass es selbst dauerhaft unter Beobachtung steht. Die Situation insbesondere deshalb so prekär, weil 'Snowman' Details enthält, die sehr aktuell und in hohem Maße politisch aufgeladen sind. Am linken Rand der Senke im Vordergrund schlagen die Schatten im Schnee plötzlich um in das anamorphotische Porträt des amerikanischen Präsidenten George W. Bush. Es kehrt nochmals wieder als Spiegelung auf der Brille des am Boden sitzenden Snowboarders. Ihm entspricht auf der gegenüber liegenden Seite zwischen den Wagenspuren das Bildnis von Ahmed Chalabi, dem ehemaligen Favoriten der US-Regierung als Chef der irakischen Übergangsregierung nach dem Sturz von Saddam Hussein. Sogleich öffnet sich eine weitere Lesart des Gemäldes: Zeigt es vielleicht nicht so sehr eine Schnee-, als vielmehr eine Wüstenlandschaft, und stammen die tiefen Spuren möglicherweise von Militärfahrzeugen? Ein weiterer Widerspruch, der kaum zu entwirren ist.

'Do you know what you are looking at?' hat Mark Tansey an den Rand der Collage für 'Snowman' geschrieben. Er formuliert damit eine Frage, die den wunden Punkt unseres von Bildern aller Art geprägten Zeitalters berührt. Wie gehen wir mit den visuellen Angeboten um, mit denen wir Tag für Tag überflutet werden? Wie verhalten wir uns zu den unzähligen Bildern, die um unsere Aufmerksamkeit buhlen, die vorgeben Informationen zu vermitteln, tatsächlich aber nicht selten Desinformation bemänteln? Sind Bilder unschuldig und sind sie Medien auch in dem Sinne, dass sie verlässliche Mittler zur Welt sind? Verstehen wir, was sie uns zu sagen haben, und wenn ja: vertrauen wir ihnen?[9] Mark Tanseys neue Arbeiten liefern – aus der inneren Dynamik seines Werks heraus – einen wesentlichen Beitrag zur Diskussion um den 'Iconoclash', um den Kampf der Bilder, der sich mit jedem neuen Fernsehkanal und jeder neuen Internetplattform weiter verschärft. Sie stellen hohe Ansprüche an den Betrachter, fordern ihn auf zu einem reflektierten Sehen und brechen seine Passivität auf mit den spezifischen Möglichkeiten der Malerei: ihrer materiellen Präsenz, Intensität und Stille.

---

another possible interpretation of the painting. Does it depict not so much a snow landscape as a desert? Were the deep tracks possibly made by military vehicles? Yet another contradiction that can hardly be resolved.

'Do you know what you are looking at?' Mark Tansey wrote on the edge of the collage for 'Snowman', immediately putting his finger on the sore point of our image-saturated age. How do we cope with the flood of images that inundates our lives day in, day out? How do we relate to those countless images that seek our attention, claim to be informative and yet are not infrequently disinformative? Are images innocent and are they also media in the sense that they are a reliable bridge to the outside world? Do we understand what they have to say, and if so, do we trust them?[9] Not least through their inner dynamism, Mark Tansey's new paintings make a vital contribution to the discussion on the 'iconoclash', the image war which intensifies with every new TV channel, with every new internet platform. They make heavy demands on the viewer, making him adopt a contemplative way of seeing and challenging his passivity with the specific possibilities of painting: its material presence, its intensity and its tranquillity.

Ich danke Mark Tansey für seine großzügige und rückhaltlose Unterstützung bei der Vorbereitung dieses Textes.

26

¹ Zit. n. Max Imdahl, Cézanne – Braque – Picasso: Zum Verhältnis zwischen Bildautonomie und Gegenstandssehen, in: ders., Reflexion – Theorie – Methode, Gesammelte Schriften, Bd. 3, hrsg. v. Gottfried Boehm, Frankfurt a.M. 1996, S. 303ff., hier: S. 309f.

² Vgl. Douglas Crimp, Das Ende der Malerei (1981), in: ders., Über die Ruinen des Museums. Mit einem photographischen Essay von Louise Lawler, Dresden / Basel 1996, S. 100ff.

³ Mark Tansey, Notes and Comments, in: Arthur C. Danto, Mark Tansey: Visions and Revisions, New York 1992, S. 127ff., hier: S. 128 (On monochrome).

⁴ Mark Tansey, Notizen, August / September 2004.

⁵ Mark Tansey im Gespräch mit dem Autor, August 2004.

⁶ Seamus Dean, Introduction, in: James Joyce, Finnegans Wake, London 2000, S. viiff., hier: S. vii.

⁷ Die Konsequenz, mit der Tansey dabei vorgeht, erinnert stark an Vexierbilder der Renaissance, etwa von Erhard Schön (um 1530). Auch dort entsteht eine Landschaft aus den anamorphotisch verzeichneten Gesichtern historischer Persönlichkeiten und muss in einem aufwändigen Leseprozess entziffert werden.

⁸ Mark Tansey im Gespräch mit dem Autor, August 2004.

⁹ Vgl. Bruno Latour, What is Iconoclash? Or is There a World Beyond the Image Wars?, in: Kat.d.Ausst. 'Iconoclash – Beyond the Image Wars in Science, Religion, and Art', hrsg. v. Bruno Latour u. Peter Weibel, Karlsruhe (Zentrum für Kunst und Medien) 2002, S. 14ff.

I wish to thank Mark Tansey for his generous and unreserved help and support during my preparations for the writing of this essay.

¹ Quoted from: Max Imdahl, Cézanne – Braque – Picasso: Zum Verhältnis zwischen Bildautonomie und Gegenstandssehen, in: idem, Reflexion – Theorie – Methode, Gesammelte Schriften, Bd. 3, edited by Gottfried Boehm, Frankfurt a.M. 1996, p. 303ff., here: p. 309f.

² Cf. Douglas Crimp, The End of Painting (1981), in: idem, On the Museum's Ruins, Cambridge, Massachusetts 1993, pp. 92-93.

³ Mark Tansey: Notes and Comments, in: Arthur C. Danto, Mark Tansey: Visions and Revisions, New York 1992, p. 127ff., here: p. 128 (On monochrome).

⁴ Mark Tansey, Notes, August / September 2004.

⁵ Mark Tansey in conversation with the author, August 2004.

⁶ Seamus Dean, Introduction, in: James Joyce, Finnegans Wake, London 2000, p. viiff., here: p. vii.

⁷ The consistency of Tansey's treatment of this theme reminds one very much of Renaissance puzzle-pictures, such as the paintings of Erhard Schön (circa 1530), for example, in which landscapes are formed from the anamorphically distorted faces of famous people of history, recognizable only through painstaking perusal.

⁸ Mark Tansey in conversation with the author, August 2004.

⁹ Cf. Bruno Latour, What is Iconoclash? Or is There a World Beyond the Image Wars?, in: exh. cat. Iconoclash – Beyond the Image Wars in Science, Religion, and Art, edited by Bruno Latour and Peter Weibel, Karlsruhe (Zentrum für Kunst und Medien) 2002, p. 14ff.

'Mont Sainte-Victoire', 1987
Öl auf Leinwand / *oil on canvas*
254 x 393,7 cm, Daros Collection,
Schweiz / *Switzerland*

Man sieht, was man weiß –
Mark Tanseys Allegorien der Moderne
Daniela Goeller

Eine mächtige Brücke überspannt den cartesianischen Abgrund, Michelangelos Jüngstes Gericht wird mit weißer Farbe überstrichen und damit ein Triumph über die Meisterschaft errungen, eine Gruppe von Sonntagsmalern hat die Staffeleien im Freien aufgestellt und hält einen Raketenstart als Action Painting fest, ein Mann geht auf dem Wasser und entzaubert so den Mythos der Tiefe, ein anderer blickt statt aus dem Fenster in einen blinden Spiegel und spricht damit das Urteil von Paris, Eskimos und Beduinen begegnen sich in der Unbestimmtheit ihrer weiß-auf-weiß ineinander übergehenden, aber klimatisch vollkommen entgegen gesetzten Lebensräume – die Gemälde von Mark Tansey werfen trotz ihrer scheinbar harmlosen Gegenständlichkeit eine Menge Fragen auf. Was dargestellt wird, ist deutlich zu erkennen, aber worum es dabei geht, erschließt sich dem Betrachter nicht ohne weiteres. Höchst rätselhafte Bilddetails liefern mehr oder weniger deutliche Indizien für eine potentielle Deutung. Wer einmal in die verlockende ikonographische Falle tappt und versucht, die visuellen Metaphern der Gemälde zu entschlüsseln, kann sich auf eine Reihe von abenteuerlichen Wendungen und unerwarteten Pointen gefasst machen. Denn der Künstler lockt den Betrachter in eine komplexe Welt bildkünstlerischer und kunsttheoretischer Reflexion.

In den 1980er Jahren gilt Mark Tanseys Interesse vor allem der Moderne und den künstlerischen Avantgarden des 20. Jahrhunderts. Dabei bedient er sich gerne der begrifflich nahe liegenden Metapher des Militärischen und stellt die Künstler als Soldaten dar, die sich einen erbitterten Kampf um bildnerische Errungenschaften und die Vorreiterrolle in einer auf Fortschritt ausgerichteten Kunstwelt liefern. Auf einem Gemälde besetzen Soldaten in wilhelminischer

Believing is Seeing – Mark Tansey's Allegories of Modernism *Daniela Goeller*

A huge bridge spans the Cartesian gap, Michelangelo's Last Judgement is painted over with white paint as a triumph over mastery, a group of Sunday painters have set up their easels in the open air in order to capture the launching of a rocket as an action painting, a man walks on water and, in so doing, demystifies the myth of depth, another looks not through a window but through a clouded mirror and pronounces the judgement of Paris, Inuits and Bedouins meet in the uncertainty of their intermerging, white on white, yet climatically disparate environments – for all their seemingly harmless objective realism, the paintings of Mark Tansey give rise to a great many questions. What they represent is clearly recognizable, but what they actually mean is by no means immediately clear to the viewer. Enigmatic details furnish more or less obvious clues for a potential interpretation. But anyone who tentatively ventures into any one of these tempting iconographical traps in an attempt at deciphering its visual metaphors must be prepared for one adventurous and unexpected twist and turn after another. For the artist lures the viewer into a complex world of aesthetic and art-theoretical reflection.

During the 1980s, Mark Tansey was interested primarily in modernism and the artistic avant-gardes of the 20th century. Enlarging upon the metaphor of the avant-garde in its military sense, Tansey represented artists as soldiers fighting a bitter battle with one another for artistic supremacy in an art world geared to the onward march of progress. In one of his paintings ('Occupation', 1984), German soldiers in First World War uniforms occupy the New York gallery district of SoHo. In another painting, four apocalyptic horsemen gallop across mud-trodden fragments of works of art of bygone centuries and different cultures. But the horsemen are standing on their heads, as reflections in a puddle, sitting on their horses the wrong way round and looking backwards through their binoculars ('Forward Retreat', 1986).

Uniform das New Yorker Galerienviertel SoHo ('Occupation', 1984), und auf einem anderen Gemälde galoppieren vier apokalyptische Reiter in Uniform über die Bruchstücke der im Schlamm zertretenen Kunstwerke früherer Jahrhunderte und unterschiedlicher Kulturkreise hinweg. Doch die Reiter sind auf dem Kopf stehend, als Spiegelung in einer Pfütze dargestellt, sie sitzen verkehrt herum auf ihren Pferden und blicken rückwärts durch ihre Ferngläser ('Forward Retreat', 1986).

Mit 'Triumph of the New York School' (1984) erhebt Tansey den Kampf der amerikanischen Avantgarde um die Vorreiterrolle in der Kunst des 20. Jahrhunderts in den Rang eines Historiengemäldes. Die als Soldaten verkleideten amerikanischen und französischen Künstler stehen sich hier am Ende der kriegerischen Auseinandersetzungen im Halbkreis gegenüber, um auf dem verwüsteten Schlachtfeld der Unterzeichnung der Urkunde über Sieg und Niederlage durch ihre Anführer beizuwohnen. An dem kleinen, mit einem Tuch bedeckten Tisch in der Bildmitte stehen sich die beiden Heerführer gegenüber. Aus der von Mark Tansey angefertigten Bildlegende geht hervor, dass es sich um den surrealistischen Schriftsteller André Breton und den amerikanischen Kunstkritiker Clement Greenberg handelt. Während sich hinter Breton die herausragenden Vertreter der französischen Avantgarde von 1850 bis 1940 versammeln, darunter Henri Matisse, Salvador Dalí, Pablo Picasso und Marcel Duchamp, ist auf der Gegenseite die amerikanische Avantgarde von 1940 bis 1950 u.a. mit Jackson Pollock, Willem de Kooning, Barnett Newman, Mark Rothko vertreten.

Versucht man das Gemälde im herkömmlichen Sinne zu deuten, stößt man auf eine ganze Reihe von Widersprüchen. Allein aus den von Tansey angegebenen Namen der dargestellten Personen ergeben sich für das Zusammentreffen schon zahlreiche Anachronismen. Auch die unterschiedliche Bekleidung der beiden Gruppen mit Uniformen aus den beiden zeitlich auseinander liegenden Weltkriegen des 20. Jahrhunderts unterstreicht das. Das Bild wird erst lesbar, wenn man es als Simultandarstellung betrachtet und das Augenmerk nicht so sehr auf die Identität der einzelnen Personen als vielmehr auf das, was sie verkörpern, richtet. Hier tritt sozusagen der Abstrakte Expressionismus gegen die

---

Tansey's 'Triumph of the New York School' (1984) places the struggle of the American avant-garde for leadership in the art of the 20th century on a par with events one would normally find depicted in a history painting. Dressed as soldiers, American and French artists stand opposite one another in a semi-circle on a devastated battlefield. The hostilities now over, they are about to witness the signing of the treaty of surrender by their respective leaders. The two generals of the opposing armies face each other across a small, cloth-covered table in the centre of the painting. They are, according to Mark Tansey's caption, the surrealist writer André Breton and the American art critic Clement Greenberg. Gathered behind Breton are the outstanding representatives of the French avant-garde from 1850 to 1940, including Henri Matisse, Salvador Dalí, Pablo Picasso and Marcel Duchamp, while the opposite camp comprises the American avant-garde from 1940 to 1950, represented by, among others, Jackson Pollock, Willem de Kooning, Barnett Newman and Mark Rothko.

Now if we attempted to interpret this painting in the conventional sense, we would discover no end of contradictions, not least on account of the identities of the depicted persons as indicated by Tansey, for they are for the most part anachronistic in the context of this gathering. These anachronisms are underlined by the fact that the two groups are wearing uniforms from two completely different epochs – the two world wars of the 20th century. The painting does not become 'readable' until we view it as a simultaneous representation and give our attention not so much to the identities of the depicted individuals but rather to what they personify, namely American Abstract Expressionism on the one hand, and the entirety of French literary and artistic modernism on the other. Viewed historically, the French avant-gardes do indeed belong in the first half of the 20th century, while the American avant-garde did not appear on the scene until after the Second World War. But then this historical factuality is upset by one contradiction after another. The conventional arrangement of the victors on the right and the defeated on the left underlines the meaning

gesamte literarische und bildkünstlerische französische Moderne an. Tatsächlich sind die französischen Avantgarden historisch in der ersten Hälfte des 20. Jahrhunderts anzusiedeln, während die amerikanische Avantgarde erst nach dem Zweiten Weltkrieg auftritt. Aber es stellen sich noch mehr Widersprüche ein. Die konventionelle Verteilung von Siegern und Verlierern auf der rechten und linken Seite unterstützt vordergründig die durch den Titel suggerierte Deutung des Bildes, die dann aber durch eine Reihe von Details relativiert wird. Die Franzosen zum Beispiel haben festen Boden unter den Füßen, während die angeblich siegreichen Amerikaner im Morast stehen.

Mark Tanseys Gemälde bieten eine Vielzahl von Möglichkeiten für eine Deutung an, und jeder dieser Ansatzpunkte bildet den Einstieg in ein Labyrinth von sich überlagernden Sinnstrukturen, die eine Vielzahl von Verbindungen und Kombinationen zulassen. Es kommt zu einer Multiplikation von Bedeutungen, die sich zu einem undurchdringlichen Geflecht verdichten. Tansey spinnt in seinen Vorarbeiten alle diese Fäden und Diskursfragmente zusammen und wählt die visuell überzeugende Umsetzung dafür. Er illustriert und karikiert hier ein kontroverses Thema der modernen und postmodernen Kunstkritik, nämlich die Behauptung, die amerikanische Avantgarde sei der europäischen Tradition überlegen.

Ein weiteres Schlüsselthema aus dem Kontext der Moderne, das Tansey mehrfach in seinen Bildern aufgreift, ist die radikale Ablehnung der Repräsentation, die sich in der Theorie von Platon über Hegel bis zu Greenberg fortsetzt. Die Argumente zu ihrer Rechtfertigung gleichen sich über Jahrhunderte hinweg: Die Nachahmung sei eine Täuschung und als solche der Wahrheit entgegengesetzt. Sie appelliere an die Sinneswahrnehmung und rufe Emotionen hervor, die den Verstand außer Kraft setzten. Dazu gesellt sich noch ein weiteres Diktum, das auch alle narrativen Aspekte aus der Kunst verbannt. In Greenbergs Augen musste sich die Malerei dazu noch Stück für Stück von der illusionistischen Darstellung des Tiefenraumes befreien, bevor sie in der Affirmation der Fläche durch die Künstler des amerikanischen abstrakten Expressionismus ihren Höhe-

---

of the painting as suggested by the title, but only superficially, for here, too, we are confronted by a great many relativizing details. The defeated French, for example, have firm ground under their feet, while the supposedly victorious Americans are standing in a quagmire.

Mark Tansey's paintings offer the viewer a multitude of possibilities for interpretation, each one of them opening a hatch leading down into a veritable labyrinth of superposed layers of meaning, these in turn permitting a multitude of associations and combinations. The result is a dense, complex and impenetrable fabric of possible interpretations. Before he begins a painting, Tansey spins all the threads and weaves all the fragments of meaning together, at the same time deciding how to achieve the visually most convincing effect. In the above-described painting, Tansey illustrates and caricatures a controversial theme of modern and post-modern art criticism, namely the assertion that the American avant-garde is superior to the European tradition. Another key theme in the context of modernism, which Tansey takes up in many of his paintings,

is the continued radical rejection of representation in art, by theorists throughout the history of art, from Plato through Hegel to Greenberg. The arguments in its defence have been much the same down the centuries: mimesis is an illusion and, as such, the opposite of truth. It appeals to the senses and evokes emotions which render reason ineffective. Added to this is a further dictum which banishes all narrative aspects from art as well. In Greenberg's eyes, painting still had to free itself bit by bit from the illusionistic representation of depth before it could finally reach its climax in the celebration of flatness by the exponents of American Abstract Expressionism. To begin with, Mark Tansey reverses this development, his adoption of a representational style and his use of allegories and metaphors in themselves already constituting a form of ideological criticism. The visual irony lies not least in the fact that he exposes the rejection of the representational with the very means of representation and uses allegory to demonstrate an art form which categorically rejects allegory.

Studie zu / *Study for* 'Occupation', 1984
Öl auf Leinwand / *oil on canvas*
66 x 96,5 cm, Daros Collection,
Schweiz / *Switzerland*

punkt erreichen konnte. Mark Tansey macht alle diese Schritte erst einmal rückgängig. Seine Hinwendung zur gegenständlichen Malerei und Repräsentation, seine Verwendung von Allegorien und Metaphern stellt also an sich bereits eine Form von Ideologiekritik dar. Der Bildwitz rührt mit daher, dass er die Ablehnung der Repräsentation mit den Mitteln der Repräsentation bloßstellt und Allegorien verwendet, um eine Kunst vorzuführen, die Allegorien kategorisch ablehnt.

Die Lichtmetaphorik, über die er einen direkten Bezug zu Platons Höhlengleichnis herstellen kann, ist ein zentrales Motiv in verschiedenen Gemälden, mit denen er diese Themen auch inhaltlich aufgreift. Auf dem Bild mit dem Titel 'Veil' (1987) erweitert er das Motiv um die Metaphorik des Schleiers, der zur Zeit der französischen Aufklärung der Wahrheit heruntergerissen werden sollte. Auf dem Gemälde 'The Bricoleur's Daughter' (1987) ist ein junges Mädchen mit einer Taschenlampe zu sehen. Auf der Kante einer Kiste balancierend, erforscht das Kind eine in vollkommenem Dunkel liegende Werkstatt, die mit allerlei Gegenständen angefüllt ist, die sonderbare Schatten an die Wand werfen. Das Gemälde wurde noch im Jahr seiner Entstehung in Kassel auf der documenta 8 gezeigt, zusammen mit 'Judgement of Paris II' (1987) und 'Mont Sainte-Victoire' (1987).

Das komplexe Thema dieses Bildes wurde von Tansey mehrmals unter Verwendung verschiedener Motive ausgeführt. Er reflektiert hier die Entstehung der Moderne zu Beginn des 20. Jahrhunderts in Zusammenhang mit den dekonstruktivistischen Denkmodellen der französischen Philosophie in der zweiten Hälfte des 20. Jahrhunderts.

Das Gemälde teilt sich oberhalb und unterhalb der spiegelglatten Wasseroberfläche in zwei Hälften. Vor der im Hintergrund deutlich zu erkennenden Kulisse des Mont Sainte-Victoire, den Paul Cézanne immer wieder gemalt hat und der so zu einer Ikone der Moderne geworden ist, befindet sich eine Gruppe von Badenden. Dieses Motiv stellt eine Hommage an ein weiteres Schlüsselwerk von Cézanne dar. Die Szene scheint sich im Wasser zu spiegeln, doch der erste

---

The allegory of light, via which Tansey establishes a direct association with Plato's Allegory of the Cave, is a central theme – in terms of both form and content – of various paintings. In 'Veil' (1987), Tansey extends the scope of this theme to include the allegory of the veil, the symbol of the impediment to truth in the French Enlightenment. His painting 'The Bricoleur's Daughter' (1987) depicts a young girl with an electric torch. Balanced on the edge of a wooden box, the child is exploring a workshop in complete darkness. The workshop is full of all kinds of objects which cast strange shadows on the wall. Painted in 1987, 'The Bricoleur's Daughter' was exhibited in the same year at documenta 8 in Kassel, together with 'Judgement of Paris II' (1987) and 'Mont Sainte-Victoire' (1987).

The complex theme of this last-named painting is one which recurs in the form of different motifs in several of Tansey's paintings. Tansey reflects here on the genesis of modernism at the beginning of the 20th century in terms of the deconstructivist thought models of French philosophy of the second half of the 20th century. The painting is divided into two halves above and below a smooth, unrippled expanse of water. Depicted against the background formed by the clearly recognizable Mont Sainte-Victoire, a motif which Paul Cézanne painted again and again and which has thus become one of the icons of modernism, is a group of bathers – a motif which likewise pays homage to another of Cézanne's key works. The scene seems to be reflected in the water, but this initial impression is deceptive: the reflections of the men bathing in the water have metamorphosed into naked women, while the mountain has turned into the Platonic Cave. It is into this scene, which can be turned upside down, like a rebus, but without giving its secret away, that Tansey introduces the philosophers Jean Baudrillard, Roland Barthes and Jacques Derrida as its observers. Thus the painting spans the divide between one of the father figures of French modernism and the deconstructivism of Derrida. The question concerning truth in art links Derrida with Cézanne, but Derrida, recognizing the unattainability of truth, turns his back on Plato.

'Veil', 1987
Öl auf Leinwand / *oil on canvas*
163 x 127 cm, Daros Collection,
Schweiz / *Switzerland*

Eindruck täuscht: Die badenden Männer verwandeln sich im Wasser in nackte Frauen, der Berg wird zur platonischen Höhle. Tansey lässt hier die Philosophen Jean Baudrillard, Roland Barthes und Jacques Derrida als Beobachter in einem Bild auftreten, das sich wie ein Rebus auf den Kopf stellen lässt, allerdings ohne seine Auflösung preiszugeben. Das Bild spannt einen Bogen von einer der Vaterfiguren der französischen Moderne zum Dekonstruktivismus Derridas, den die Frage nach der Wahrheit in der Kunst mit Cézanne verbindet, der sich aber in der Erkenntnis der Unerreichbarkeit dieser Wahrheit von Platon abwendet.

Tansey hat sich wie viele Künstler seiner Generation intensiv mit Philosophie und Kunsttheorie auseinandergesetzt. Sein Weg zurück zum Bild vollzieht sich über diese Auseinandersetzung. Die Lösung liegt für ihn darin, genau diese Themen zu seinen Bildinhalten zu machen. Er findet in der Allegorie das adäquate Verfahren, seine Ideen in Bilder umzusetzen. Für Tansey existiert das Bild unabhängig von einer abzubildenden Realität. Er verbindet Elemente im Bild, die aus unterschiedlichen Kontexten stammen und unterschiedlichen Zeitepochen angehören, in einer Fläche. Dieser Schritt ist in jeder Hinsicht anti-avantgardistisch. Er stellt nicht nur einen (zeitlichen) Rückschritt dar, sondern bricht mit dem für die Avantgarde ausschlaggebenden Kriterium des Neuen und der Originalität. Stattdessen führt er zur Selbstreflexion der Malerei. Tansey versinnbildlicht kunsttheoretische Fragestellungen und zeigt damit Grenzen auf – für die Kunst und für die Kunsttheorie. Die dabei von ihm benutzten Allegorien sind nicht unbedingt allgemeinverständlich, d.h. man muss entweder die Hintergründe sehr genau kennen oder sie sich erklären lassen. Es geht bei Tansey aber gar nicht so sehr darum, dass der Betrachter noch das letzte Bilddetail versteht. Die Allegorie ist vielmehr als Verfahren wichtig, weil sie es Tansey ermöglicht, nach dem angeblichen Ende der Malerei wieder ein Bild zu malen.

Wer mit dem Mikrophon in der Hand vor den Lippen einer Sphinx kniet und die Lösung ihres Geheimnisses mit dem Tonbandgerät aufzeichnen will, hat alles und nichts verstanden. Man sieht zwar, was man weiß, aber man kann diese Bilder auch erfassen, ohne von allem zu wissen, was man sieht.

Like many artists of his generation, Mark Tansey has concerned himself intensively with philosophy and art theory. Indeed, it was this concern that led him back to the painted picture. His solution was to make precisely these themes the subject matter of his paintings and to use allegory as a means of expressing his ideas visually. For Tansey, the painted picture exists independently of any depictable reality. His paintings combine, in the same picture plane, pictorial elements belonging to different contexts and different epochs, a step which is altogether anti-avant-garde, for not only is it a step taken backwards in time, but it also breaks with the decisive avant-garde criterion of newness and originality. Instead, the painting becomes self-reflexive; it symbolizes art-theoretical questions and defines the limits, both of art and of art theory. The allegories used by Tansey to this end are not necessarily intelligible to all, and if one is not fully conversant with the background, it will require explanation. However, Tansey is not all that concerned about the viewer's understanding of his paintings down to the last detail. The allegory is more important to Tansey as a process, because it enables him – after the alleged demise of painting as an art form – to paint pictures again.

Any one reverently holding a microphone to the lips of a sphinx in the hope of recording the answer to its riddle on tape understands everything and nothing. One sees what one knows, but one can also understand these paintings without knowing all about everything one sees.

Tafeln

Plates

'Push-Pull', 2002
Öl auf Leinwand / *oil on canvas*
213 x 277 cm, Collection
Danielle and David Ganek

'Wake', 2003
Öl auf Leinwand / *oil on canvas*
217 x 244 cm, The Broad Art
Foundation, Santa Monica

'West Face', 2004
Öl auf Leinwand / *oil on canvas*
213 x 213 cm, Collection Donald B.
Marron, Lightyear Capital, New York

'West Face', 2004 (Details / *details*)

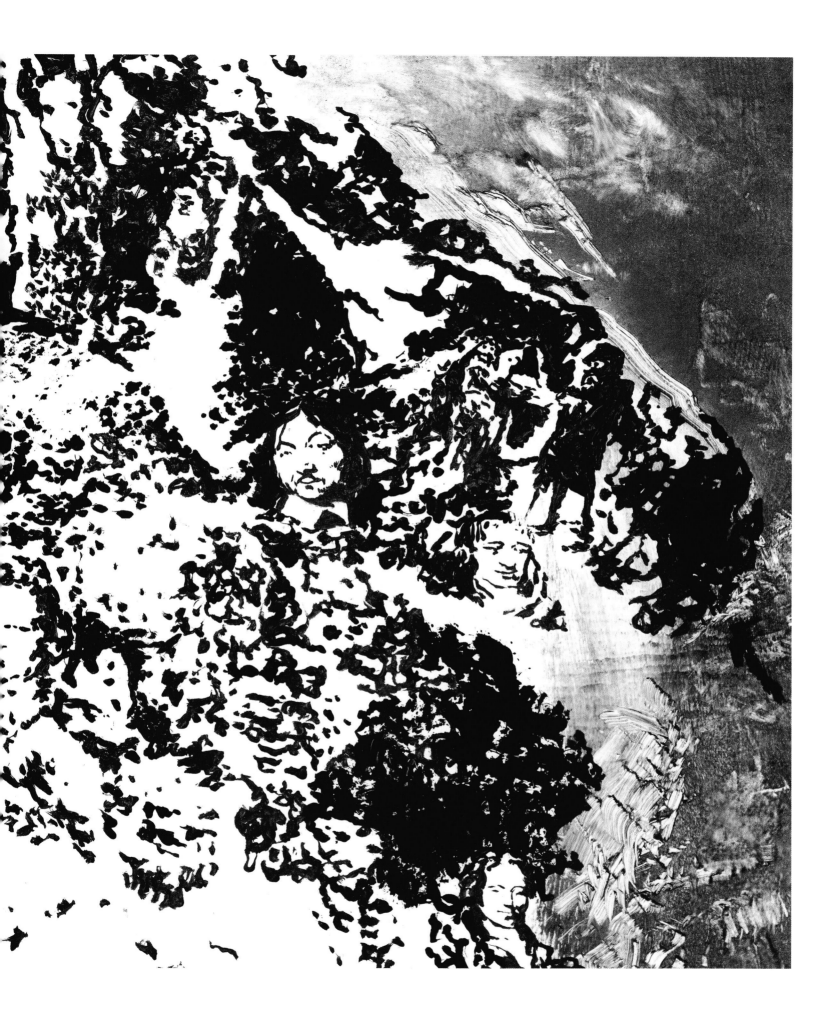

'Snowman', 2004
Öl auf Leinwand / *oil on canvas*
163 x 184 cm, Privatsammlung /
Private collection, Courtesy
Gagosian Gallery, New York

'Duet', 2004
Öl auf Leinwand / *oil on canvas*
213 x 213 cm, Courtesy Gagosian
Gallery, New York

'Sea Change', 2005
Öl auf Leinwand / *oil on canvas*
213 x 152 cm, Courtesy Gagosian
Gallery, New York

'Trio', 2004
Öl auf Leinwand / *oil on
canvas,* 217 x 356 cm
The Schroeder Collection

Studien

Studies

Collage für 'Triumph of the New York School' / *Collage for 'Triumph of the New York School'*, 1984, Photokopie auf Museumskarton und Acetat-Überzug / *photocopy on museum board and acetate overlay*, 279 x 406 mm Mark Tansey, New York

Ecke West Broadway und Spring Street / *Corner of West Broadway and Spring Street*, 1983, C-Print, 203 x 305 mm Mark Tansey, New York

Reproduktion eines Photos aus dem Ersten Weltkrieg / *World War I Photo Reproduction*, undatiert / *no date*, Papier / *paper*, 114 x 171 mm, Mark Tansey, New York

A German Field Telephone in East Prussia

© *Underwood and Underwood.*

To Strengthen German Positions Threatened by the Allies

The ever freshly arriving German troops choke up the
streets of the little French villages on the Western front.

German Reinforcements Arrive in the Villages of Northern France

NEWLY ARRIVED GERMAN TROOPS PASSING THROUGH A VILLAGE OF NORTHERN FRANCE ON THEIR WAY TO THE FRONT.

Times Mid-Week Pictorial, July 13, 1916
Zeitung / *newspaper*, 210 x 267 mm,
Mark Tansey, New York

Times Mid-Week Pictorial, July 13, 1916
Zeitung / *newspaper*, 197 x 267 mm,
Mark Tansey, New York

Collage für 'Occupation' / *Collage for
'Occupation'*, Photokopie auf Museumskarton / *photocopy on museum board*,
286 x 349 mm, Mark Tansey, New York

Collagen-Studien Nr. 1-5 für 'Bathers' /
Collage study #1-5, for 'Bathers', 1985-86
Photokopie auf Papier / *photocopy on paper*, je / *each,* 279 x 432 mm, Mark
Tansey, New York

Collagen-Studie Nr. 6 für 'Bathers' /
Collage study #6 for 'Bathers', 1985-88
Photokopie auf Papier / *photocopy on
paper*, 457 x 724 mm, Mark Tansey,
New York

Collagen-Studie Nr. 3 für 'Mont Sainte-
Victoire' / *Collage study #3 for 'Mont
Sainte-Victoire'*, 1986, Photokopie auf
Papier / *photocopy on paper*
552 x 787 mm, Mark Tansey, New York

Collagen-Studie Nr. 1 für 'Mont Sainte-Victoire' / *Collage study #1 for 'Mont Sainte-Victoire'*, 1986, Photokopie auf Papier / *photocopy on paper*
203 x 298 mm, Mark Tansey, New York

Collagen-Studie Nr. 2 für 'Mont Sainte-Victoire' / *Collage study #2 for 'Mont Sainte-Victoire'*, 1986, Photokopie auf Papier / *photocopy on paper*
311 x 483 mm, Mark Tansey, New York

Collage für 'Veil', 1987 / Collage for 'Veil', 1987, Photokopie auf Papier / *photocopy on paper,* 495 x 432 mm
Mark Tansey, New York

Collage für 'Push-Pull' Nr. 2 / *Collage for
'Push-Pull' #2*, 2002, Photokopie auf
Papier / *photocopy on paper*
279 x 432 mm, Mark Tansey, New York

Collage für 'Push-Pull' Nr. 1 / *Collage for
'Push-Pull' #1*, 2001, Photokopie auf
Papier / *photocopy on paper*
241 x 238 mm, Mark Tansey, New York

Collage für 'Push-Pull' Nr. 3 / *Collage for
'Push-Pull' #3*, 2002, Photokopie auf
Papier / *photocopy on paper*
295 x 337 mm, Mark Tansey, New York

Collagen-Studie für 'Wake' / *Collage study for 'Wake'*, 2003, Photokopie auf Papier / *photocopy on paper* 356 x 406 mm, Mark Tansey, New York

Collagen-Studie für 'Wake' (Detail) / *Collage study for 'Wake' (detail)*, 2003, Photokopie auf Papier / *photocopy on paper,* 279 x 400 mm, Mark Tansey, New York

Collage für 'Snowman' / *Collage for 'Snowman'*, 2004, Photokopie auf Papier / *photocopy on paper* 279 x 432 mm, Mark Tansey, New York

Collagen-Studie für 'West Face' (Detail) / *Collage study for 'West Face' (detail)*, 2004, Photokopie auf Papier / *photocopy on paper,* 432 x 279 mm, Mark Tansey, New York

Collagen-Studie für 'West Face' / *Collage study for 'West Face'*, 2004 Photokopie auf Papier / *photocopy on paper,* 394 x 400 mm, Mark Tansey, New York

Letzte Collage für 'West Face' / *Collage (final) for 'West Face'*, 2004, Photokopie auf Papier / *photocopy on paper* 375 x 368 mm, Mark Tansey, New York

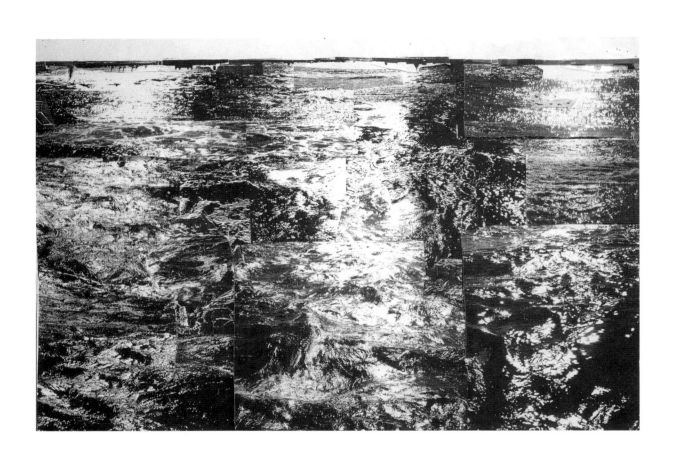

Collage für 'Trio', 2004 / *Collage for*
'Trio', 2004, Photokopie auf Papier /
photocopy on paper, 330 x 432 mm,
Mark Tansey, New York

Collagen-Studie für 'Sea Change' /
Collage study for 'Sea Change', 2004
Photokopie auf Papier / *photocopy on
paper,* 381 x 267 mm, Mark Tansey,
New York

Anhang

Appendix

Mark Tansey
1949 geboren in San José, Kalifornien /
born in San José, California
lebt und arbeitet in New York City /
lives and works in New York City

'Alteration', 1975
Gouache auf Postkarte / *gouache on
postcard*, 102 x 152 mm, Privatsammlung /
Private collection, Courtesy Gagosian
Gallery, New York

Einzelausstellungen (Auswahl) / *Solo exhibitions (selection)*

1982   New York, New York, Grace Borgenicht Gallery
1984   New York, New York, Grace Borgenicht Gallery
       San Francisco, California, John Berggruen Gallery
       Houston, Texas, Contemporary Arts Museum
1986   New York, New York, Curt Marcus Gallery
1990   New York, New York, Curt Marcus Gallery
       Basel, Kunsthalle
1990-91 Seattle, Washington, Seattle Art Museum
       (Wanderausstellung / travelling exhibition)
1992   New York, New York, Curt Marcus Gallery
1993   Los Angeles, California, Los Angeles County Museum
       of Art (Wanderausstellung / travelling exhibition)
       Los Angeles, California, Kohn / Abrams Gallery
       New York, New York, Curt Marcus Gallery
1994   Boston, Massachusetts, Museum of Fine Arts
1995   Düsseldorf, Kunstverein für die Rheinlande und
       Westfalen
       Kopenhagen / Copenhagen, Galleri Faurschou
1997   New York, New York, Curt Marcus Gallery
2000   New York, New York, Curt Marcus Gallery
2004   New York, New York, Gagosian Gallery
2005   Kleve / Cleves, Museum Kurhaus Kleve
       Stuttgart, Württembergischer Kunstverein

Gruppenausstellungen (Auswahl) / *Group exhibitions (selection)*

1978   New York, New York, Fifth Street Gallery, Artists
       of P.S. 122
1980   New York, New York, P.S. 122, Open Studio Exhibition
       New York, New York, The Drawing Center,
       Selections 12
1981   New York, New York, Grace Borgenicht Gallery, Episodes
       New York, New York, The New Museum, Not Just for
       Laughs: The Art of Subversions
1982   New York, New York, The Drawing Center, New
       Drawing in America
       Summit, New Jersey, Summit Art Center, Drawing –
       New Directions
       Indianapolis, Indiana, Indianapolis Museum of Art,
       Painting and Sculpture Today
1983   New York, New York, Museum of Modern Art, Recent
       Acquisitions
       Dallas, Texas, Carol Taylor Fine Arts, New Work /
       New York
       New York, New York, Whitney Museum of American
       Art, 1983 Biennial Exhibition
       Norfolk, Virginia, The Chrysler Museum, Reallegory
       Long Island City, New York, P.S. 1, Multiple Choice
       New York, New York, Queens Museum, 20th Century
       Art from the Metropolitan Museum of Art: Selected
       Recent Acquisitions
       New York, New York, The New Museum, Inaugural
       Exhibition
1984   Oberlin, Ohio, Allen Memorial Art Museum, Oberlin
       College, Drawings: After Photography
       (Wanderausstellung / travelling exhibition)

Boston, Massachusetts, Institute of Contemporary Art,
Currents
Fort Lauderdale, Florida, Museum of Art, Narrative
Painting: Selected Recent Acquisitions from the
Metropolitan Museum of Art
New York, New York, Tower Gallery, Body Politic
New York, New York, Museum of Modern Art, An
International Survey of Recent Painting and Sculpture
Mexico City, Museo Rufino Tamayo, Nueva pintura nar-
rativa
Los Angeles, California, Museum of Contemporary Art,
Automobile and Culture
1985   Jacksonville, Florida, Jacksonville Art Museum, The
       Figure in 20th Century Art – Selections from the
       Metropolitan Museum of Art (Wanderausstellung / tra-
       velling exhibition)
       Trenton, New Jersey, Holman Hall Art Gallery, Trenton
       State College, Contemporary Issues II
       New York, New York, Lorence-Monk Gallery, Real Surreal
       Pittsfield, Massachusetts, Berkshire Museum, Cultural
       Commentary
1986   Tokyo, Tsuromoto Room, Correspondences: New York
       Art Now
       New York, New York, Charles Cowles Annex Gallery,
       Artists for Artists
       New York, New York, Whitney Museum of American Art
       at Equitable Center, Figure as Subject: The Last Decade
       New York, New York, Curt Marcus Gallery, Inaugural
       Exhibition
       New York, New York, CDS Gallery, Artists Choose Artists IV
       New York, New York, One Penn Plaza, Short Stories
       Venedig / Venice, Biennale / Biennial, Aperto 86
       New York, New York, City Gallery, Cinemaobject
       San Francisco, California, San Francisco Museum of
       Modern Art, Second Sight: Biennial IV
       New York, New York, Sherry French Gallery,
       Telling Art
       New York, New York, Lorence-Monk Gallery, The
       Manor in the Landscape
       Purchase, New York, Neuberger Museum at the State
       University of New York, The Window in Twentieth-
       Century Art
1987   New York, New York, Barbara Toll Fine Arts, Monsters:
       The Phenomena of Dispassion
       Chicago, Gallery 400, University of Illinois at Chicago,
       Tragic and Timeless Today: Contemporary History
       Painting
       Stamford, Connecticut, Whitney Museum of American
       Art, Contemporary Diptychs: Divided Visions
       (Wanderausstellung / travelling exhibition)
       Los Angeles, California, Los Angeles County Museum
       of Art, Avant-Garde in the Eighties
       New York, New York, Museum of Modern Art, Art
       Advisory Service Exhibition, exhibited at the American
       Express Company, Utopian Visions
       Miami, Florida, The Art Museum at Florida Interna-
       tional University, American Art Today: The Portrait
       Kassel, documenta 8
       New York, New York, Curt Marcus Gallery / Kent Fine
       Art, Fictions: A Selection of Pictures from the 18th,
       19th, and 20th Centuries

1987-89 Philadelphia, Pennsylvania, Moore College of Art, Morality Tales: History Painting in the 1980s (Wanderausstellung / travelling exhibition)

1988 Trenton, New Jersey, Holman Hall Art Gallery, Trenton State College, Bleckner, Richter, Tansey: Works from the Collection of Robert M. Kaye
New York, New York, Queens Museum, Classical Myth and Imagery in Contemporary Art
New York, New York, Marlborough Gallery, Visions / Revisions: Contemporary Representation
Long Beach, California, Long Beach Museum of Art, Selections from the Berkus Collection
Santa Monica, California, Eli Broad Family Foundation, Inaugural Exhibition
Miami, Florida, The Art Museum at Florida International University, American Art Today: Narrative Painting
New York, New York, Curt Marcus Gallery, Works on Paper

1989 New York, New York, P.P.O.W., Broken Landscape, Discarded Object
Frankfurt a.M., Kunstverein, Prospect 89
Los Angeles, California, Thomas Solomon's Garage, The Observatory

1989-90 Fort Worth, Texas, Modern Art Museum of Fort Worth, 10 + 10: Contemporary Soviet and American Painters (Wanderausstellung / travelling exhibition)
Tokyo, National Museum of Modern Art, Color and / or Monochrome (Wanderausstellung / travelling exhibition)
New York, New York, Whitney Museum of American Art, Image World: Art and Media Culture

1989-91 Perth, Art Gallery of Western Australia, Romance and Irony in Recent American Art (Wanderausstellung / travelling exhibition)

1990 New York, New York, Shea & Becker, In the Realm of the Plausible
New York, New York, Edward Thorp Gallery, Storyline
Richmond, Virginia, Museum of Fine Arts, Harmony and Discord: American Landscape Painting Today
Paris, Galerie Thaddaeus Ropac, Vertigo
New York, New York, Whitney Museum of American Art, Downtown Branch, The Charade of Mastery: Deciphering Modernism in Contemporary Art

1991 New York, New York, Lorence-Monk Gallery, Dead Heroes, Disfigured Love
New York, New York, Whitney Museum of American Art, 1991 Biennial Exhibition
New York, New York, Curt Marcus Gallery
Hartford, Connecticut, Real Art Ways, The Fetish of Knowledge
New York, New York, Josh Baer Gallery, The Library

1992 Union, New Jersey, James Howe Gallery, Kean College of New Jersey, The Word-Image in Contemporary Art
Bennington, Vermont, Suzanne Lemberg Usdan Gallery, Bennington College, Representation – Reproduction – Production: The Work of Art in the Age of Mechanical Reproduction
Ridgefield, Connecticut, The Aldrich Museum of Contemporary Art, Quotations: The Second History of Art

1993 New York, New York, Grey Art Gallery, New York University, Brief Encounters: Meeting in Art
New York, New York, Thread Waxing Space, I am the Enunciator

1994 Aspen, Colorado, Aspen Art Museum, Mountains of the Mind
Denver, Colorado, Denver Art Museum, Landscape as a Metaphor (Wanderausstellung / travelling exhibition)
New York, New York, Curt Marcus Gallery
Kansas City, Missouri, Gallery of Art – University of Missouri, Drawings: Reaffirming the Media
Los Angeles, California, Thomas Solomon's Garage, World of Tomorrow
Boston, Museum of Fine Arts, Connections – Mark Tansey

1995 Aspen, Colorado, Aspen Art Museum, Contemporary Drawing: Exploring the Territory
Binghamton, New York, Binghamton University Art Museum, Traditional Landscapes: Mapping the Unconscious Psyche and Nonterrestrial Spaces (Wanderausstellung / travelling exhibition)

1996 Nyack, New York, Hopper House Art Center, Realism at 7 A.M.
Washington, D.C., National Museum of American Art, American Kaleidoscope
Winston-Salem, North Carolina, Southeastern Center for Contemporary Art, Heroic Painting

1997 Boston, Massachusetts, Boston University, Painting Machines: Industrial Image in Contemporary Art

1998 San Diego, California, Museum of Contemporary Art, Double Trouble: The Patchett Collection

1999 New York, New York, Paine Webber Group Inc., Art Works: The PaineWebber Collection of Contemporary Masters
Montreal, Montreal Museum of Fine Art, Cosmos: From Romanticism to the Avant-garde
Barcelona, Jóan Miro Foundation, Reality and Desire
Houston, Texas, Contemporary Arts Museum, Art at Work: Forty Years of The Chase Manhattan Collection

2000 Miami, Florida, The Art Museum at Florida International University, Modernism and Abstraction: Treasures from the Smithsonian American Museum of Art (Wanderausstellung / travelling exhibition)

2001 Miami, Florida, Miami Art Museum, American Tableaux: Selections from the Collection of Walker Art Center (Wanderausstellung / travelling exhibition)
New York, New York, Curt Marcus Gallery,
Beverly Hills, California, Michael Kohn Gallery, Inaugural Exhibition
Peking / Beijing, Yanhuang Art Museum, Re-Configuration: Works on Paper
Chicago, Illinois, Alan Koppel Gallery, Recent Acquisitions

2003 New York, New York, DFN Gallery, The Burbs
Raleigh, North Carolina, North Carolina Museum of Art, Defying Gravity: Contemporary Art and Flight

2003-04 Berlin, Martin-Gropius-Bau / Moskau, Staatliche Tretjakow-Galerie, Berlin – Moskau 1950-2000: von heute aus

2004 St. Louis, Missouri, Washington University Gallery of Art / Sam Fox Arts Center, Selections from the Broad Collections
Houston, Texas, Contemporary Arts Museum, Perspectives @ 25: A Quarter Century of New Art in Houston

Bibliographie (Auswahl) / *Bibliography (selection)*

1980 Larson, K., Constructive Criticism, in: Village Voice, 29.10.

1981 Schjeldahl, P., But Seriously, Folks …, in: Village Voice, 9.12.

1982 Kat.d.Ausst. / exh.cat. 'Mark Tansey', Text von / text by P. Frank, New York (Grace Borgenicht Gallery)
Raynor, V., Mark Tansey in First Solo Show, in: New York Times, 5.11.

1983 Friedman, J.R., Mark Tansey, in: Arts Magazine, 57, 5
[Philips, D.C.], Mark Tansey, in: ArtNews, 82, 1
Zelevansky, L., Mark Tansey, in: Flash Art, 110
Armstrong, R., Mark Tansey, in: Artforum, 21, 6
Owens, C., Mark Tansey, in: Art in America, 71, 2
Philips, D.C., Mark Tansey, in: ArtNews, 82, 2

1984 Freeman, P. (u. a.), New Art, New York

1986 Saltz, J. / Smith, R. / Halley, P., Beyond Boundaries: New York's New Art, New York
Martin, R., 'Rust Is What Our Metal Substitutes for Tears': The New Paintings of Mark Tansey, in: Arts Magazine, 60, 9
Russell, J., Mark Tansey, in: New York Times, 2.5.
Cameron, D., Report from the Front, in: Arts Magazine, 60, 10
Cone, M., Mark Tansey, in: Flash Art, 129
Kuspit, D., Mark Tansey, in: Artforum, 25, 1
Heartney, E., Mark Tansey, in: ArtNews, 85, 8

1987 Blau, D., Where the Telephone Never Rings: Tansey's 'Conversation', 1986, in: Parkett, 13
McCormick, C., Fracts of Life, in: Artforum, 25, 5
Johnson, A., The Death of Ethnigraphy, in: Sciences, 27, 2
Martin, R., Cézanne's Doubt and Mark Tansey's Certainty on Considering 'Mont Sainte-Victoire', in: Arts Magazine, 62, 3

1988 Kandel, S., Hayt-Atkins, E., Mark Tansey, in: ArtNews, 87, 1
Holert, T., Mark Tansey und seine Bilder, in: Wolkenkratzer Art Journal, 1
Mahoney, R., Fictions, in: Arts Magazine, 62, 6
Martin, R., Fictions: Mark Tansey's 'Triumph over Mastery', in: Arts Magazine, 62, 6
Perl, J., From September to December, in: New Criterion, 6, 6
Albig, J.-U., Ein Denker malt Kritik, in: Art, 4
Cokke, L., Fictions, in: Artscribe, 70
Joselit, D., Mark Tansey, in: Bijutsu Techo, 40
Metken, G., Attacken gegen die Avantgarde: Mark Tansey, ein Historienmaler der Postmoderne, in: Frankfurter Allgemeine Zeitung, 8.10.

1989 Hjort, Ø., Kunst, Kitsch, Überkitsch: Nogle af 80-ernes amerkanske Kunstnere, in: Kritik, 88
Pincus-Witten, R., Entries: Concentrated Juice & Kitschy Kitschy Koons, in: Arts Magazine, 63, 6
Cantor, J., La rueda de la fortuna / Wheel of Fortune, in: Arena International Art, 3
Holz, H.H., Andy Warhol: Vom Mechanismus des Erfolgs, in: Artis, 41, 7-8
Hughes, R., Mucking with Media, in: Time, 25

1990 Kat.d.Ausst. / exh.cat., 'Mark Tansey: Art and Source', Text von / text by P. Sims, Seattle (Seattle Art Museum)
Kat.d.Ausst. / exh.cat., 'Mark Tansey', Texte von / texts by G. Metken, T. Kellein, Basel (Kunsthalle)
Grundberg, A., Crisis of the Real: Writings on Photography, 1974-1989
Wolf, B., What the Cow Saw, or, Nineteenth-Century Art and the Innocent Eye, in: Antiques, 137, 1
Murray, K., Romance and Irony, in: Art & Text, 36
Miller, J., Mark Tansey, in: Artforum, 28, 10
Danto, A.C., The State of the Art World: The Nineties Begin, in: Nation, 9.7.
Grundberg, A., Attacking Not Only Masters but Mastery as Well, in: New York Times, 30. 11.

1991 Nesbitt, L.E., Mark Tansey, in: Artforum, 29, 7
Patin, T., Up and Down the Theory Ladder: Mark Tansey at the Seattle Art Museum, in: Artweek, 22, 10
Metken, G., Mark Tansey, in: Flash Art, 159
Danto, A.C., L'Esperluète et le point d'exclamation: À propos de 'High and Low' et d' 'Art et Pub', in: Cahiers du Musée national d'art moderne, 37

1992 Danto, A.C., Mark Tansey: Visions and Revisions, New York
Holm, M.J., Maleren Mark Tansey, in: Kritik, 5, 98
Danto, A.C., Trompe l'œil, in: Nation, 4.5.
Bass, R., Mark Tansey, in: ArtNews, 91, 8

1993 Kat.d.Ausst. / exh.cat. 'Mark Tansey', Texte von / texts by J. Freeman, A. Robbe-Grillet, M. Tansey, Los Angeles (County Museum of Art)

1995 Kat.d.Ausst. / exh.cat. ''Triumph der New York School' von Mark Tansey', Texte von / texts by A.C. Danto, R. Stecker, Düsseldorf

1999 Taylor, M.C., The Picture in Question – Mark Tansey and the Ends of Representation, Chicago

2002 Scorzin, P.C., Die Malerei im Zustand ihrer geschichtlichen Reflexivität, in: Künstler, Kritisches Lexikon der Gegenwartskunst, Ausgabe 58, München

2003 Danto, A.C., Ironie als Muse – Mark Tansey, Vitaly Komar und Alexander Melamid, in: Kat.d.Ausst. / exh.cat. 'Berlin / Moskau 1950-2000: von heute aus', Berlin (Martin-Gropius-Bau)

2005 Kat.d.Ausst. / exh.cat. 'Mark Tansey', Text von / text by R. Mönig, New York (Gagosian Gallery)

Impressum / *Colophon*

Schriftenreihe Museum Kurhaus Kleve – Ewald Mataré-Sammlung Nr. 26 / *Publications of the Museum Kurhaus Kleve – Ewald Mataré-Collection No. 26*

Herausgeber / *Editor*
Freundeskreis Museum Kurhaus und Koekkoek-Haus Kleve e.V. anlässlich der Ausstellung im / *on the occasion of the exhibition at the* Museum Kurhaus Kleve, 23.1.-24.4.2005 und im / *and at the* Württembergischen Kunstverein Stuttgart, 4.5.-17.7.2005

Ausstellung und Katalog / *Exhibition and catalogue*
Mark Tansey, Roland Mönig

Redaktion / *Editing*
Roland Mönig

Photographie / *Photography*
Daros Collection, Schweiz / *Switzerland*, S. 28/29, 33, 35
Annegret Gossens, Museum Kurhaus Kleve, S. 11, 15, 19, 23
Robert McKeever, New York, Courtesy Gagosian Gallery, S. 2, 40-57, 60-77, 80, 83

Übersetzung / *Translation*
John Brogden, Dortmund

Sekretariat in Kleve / *Secretariat in Cleves*
Nicole Ramcke

Ausstellungsaufbau in Kleve / *Setup of the exhibition in Cleves*
Wilhelm Dückerhoff, Norbert van Appeldorn

Sekretariat in Stuttgart / *Secretariat in Stuttgart*
Gisela Krönke

Ausstellungsaufbau in Stuttgart / *Setup of the exhibition in Stuttgart*
Serge de Waha, Laurens Nitschke, Markus Starke

Gestaltung / *Design*
Michael Zöllner, Köln

Druck / *Printing*
B.o.s.s Druck und Medien GmbH, Kleve

Lithographie / *Colour separations*
Bildarbeit, Henning Krause, Köln

© 2005
Mark Tansey, Museum Kurhaus Kleve, Kerber Verlag Bielefeld und Autoren / *and authors*

Museumsausgabe:
Museum Kurhaus Kleve
ISBN 3-934935-20-6

Buchhandelsausgabe:
Kerber Verlag Bielefeld
ISBN 3-938025-11-5

KERBER VERLAG

Bibliographische Information der Deutschen Bibliothek
Die Deutsche Bibliothek verzeichnet diese Publikation in der Deutschen Nationalbibliographie; detaillierte bibliographische Daten sind im Internet über http://dnb.ddb.de abrufbar.

US Distribution
D.A.P., Distributed Art Publishers Inc.
155 Sixth Avenue 2nd Floor
New York, N.Y. 10013
Tel. 001 212 6 27 19 99
Fax 001 212 6 27 94 84

Die Ausstellung in Kleve wird gefördert durch
The exhibition in Cleves is supported by

kulturstiftung des bundes

KUNSTSTIFTUNG ○ NRW

Botschaft der
USA in Berlin

GEORGIA HOTEL CLEVE

Die Ausstellung in Stuttgart wird gefördert durch
The exhibition in Stuttgart is supported by

Stiftung
Landesbank Baden-Württemberg

LB≡BW

HUGO BOSS